DATE DUE

DEMCO 38-296

OC '90

GREAT WRITERS OF THE ENGLISH LANGUAGE

Great Poets

TAFF CREDITS

Executive Editor
Reg Wright

Series Editor
Sue Lyon

Editors
Jude Welton
Sylvia Goulding

Deputy Editors
Alice Peebles
Theresa Donaghey

Features Editors
Geraldine McCaughrean
Emma Foa
Ian Chilvers

Art Editors
Kate Sprawson
Jonathan Alden
Helen James

Designers
Simon Wilder
Frank Landamore

Senior Picture Researchers
Julia Hanson
Vanessa Fletcher
Georgina Barker

Picture Clerk
Vanessa Cawley

Production Controllers
Judy Binning
Tom Helsby

Editorial Secretaries
Fiona Bowser
Sylvia Osborne

Managing Editor
Alan Ross

Editorial Consultant
Maggi McCormick

Publishing Manager
Robert Paulley

Reference Edition Published 1989
Published by Marshall Cavendish Corporation
147 West Merrick Road
Freeport, Long Island
N.Y. 11520

Typeset by Litho Link Ltd., Welshpool
Printed and Bound in Italy by
L.E.G.O. S.p.a. Vicenza

LIBRARY OF CONGRESS
Library of Congress Cataloging-in-Publication Data
Great Writers of the English Language
    p. cm.
    Includes index vol.
    ISBN 1-85435-000-5 (set): $399.95
    1. English literature — History and criticism. 2. English
literature — Stories, plots, etc. 3. American literature — History
and criticism. 4. American literature — Stories, plots, etc.
5. Authors. English — Biography. 6. Authors. American — Biography.
I. Marshall Cavendish Corporation.
PR85.G66 1989
820'.9 – dc19
                         88-21077
                         CIP

ISBN 1–85435–000–5 (set)
ISBN 1–85435–013–7 (vol)

GREAT WRITERS OF THE ENGLISH LANGUAGE

Great Poets

Geoffrey Chaucer

William Shakespeare

The Romantic Poets

The War Poets

MARSHALL CAVENDISH · NEW YORK · TORONTO · LONDON · SYDNEY

CONTENTS

GEOFFREY CHAUCER

c.1340-1400

Chaucer's mental energies must have been phenomenal, his character full of contradictory virtues. He was a diplomat, tactful and discreet, yet he was called on to entertain the Court with songs and poems; he was a civil servant entrusted with important missions abroad, yet he found time to educate himself in every field of study. And all the while he was writing poetry of originality and vigour which would set his name at the very foundation of English literature.

The Perfect Courtier

As a 14th-century courtier, Chaucer was steward, statesman, soldier, poet and politician; literary genius in no way freed him from his duties to a succession of powerful masters.

It was not unusual in the Middle Ages for men to combine different strands of occupation in their lives, yet Geoffrey Chaucer's achievements, not only as the first great English poet, but as scholar, courtier, civil servant and diplomat, prove him an unusual and exceptionally gifted man. Sadly, we know a good deal about his career as a servant of the king, but virtually nothing of his personal life and character.

He was born in the early 1340s, at a time when England, with Edward III on the throne, was more stable and settled than it had been for half a century. Within a few years of his birth, England had achieved a glorious and devastating victory over the knighthood of France at the Battle of Crecy, and Edward's court was beginning to emerge as one of the most brilliant and colourful in Europe.

Chaucer's family were part of the newly rising merchant class. His great-grandfather had a tavern in Ipswich, in the county of Suffolk. But his grandfather Robert Malin le Chaucer set up a wine wholesale business in London, and made such a success of it that Chaucer's father John was able to marry a wealthy heiress, Agnes Copton, niece and ward of a 'moneyer' at the Royal Mint. The flamboyant John Chaucer had been outlawed as a ringleader of a rebel troop in the 1320s, but in 1338 went to the wars in France as a member of the King's retinue.

A PAGE AT COURT

Whole villages were wiped out by wars or by that other wholesale slaughter – the Plague or Black Death. Yet some bitter comfort was to be derived from it: shortage of labour in the country freed many serfs from their bondage, while the sudden loss of many courtiers gave the sons of ordinary merchants like Chaucer the chance to rise in the King's service. As a boy Chaucer probably went to one of London's three grammar schools, where the pupils were taught Latin grammar, and learned Latin poetry. At this time, French (the language of court) was spoken by people of any social pretension, and Chaucer would have learned it alongside his native English. He must have done well at school, for by the time he was 14 or so, he was a page in the service of the illustrious Elizabeth, Countess of Ulster, and then her husband, Prince Lionel, son of Edward III. A document dated 4

April 1357 shows that Elizabeth bought 'Galfridus Chaucer' shoes, black and red breeches and a 'paltok' (short cloak).

By 1359, he had 'received arms' and become a squire, an apprentice knight, well versed in all the arts of chivalry – fighting, paying court and Christian duty. Perhaps the picture of the squire in *The Canterbury Tales*, "a lover and a lusty bachelor", recalls Chaucer's own days as a squire. It may be that Chaucer actually fought in the French wars, for he was certainly captured by the French for a while, and released only when a ransom was paid; King Edward contributed £16.

As Lionel's squire, Chaucer witnessed the splendour and sophistication of Edward III's court at first hand, following its grand progress around the country. He must have heard fashionable French poets recite and sing their elegant romances to the

Edward III
Crowned in 1327, Edward III (above) reigned for 50 years and had six sons. He was a warrior king, but had a highly cultured court.

New wealth
John Chaucer, Geoffrey's father, returned from outlawry to inherit a new family fortune made from wine trading (below).

Key Dates

c.1340 born in London

1357 page to the Countess of Ulster

1359 captured in France and ransomed

1366 marries Philippa Roet

1367 joins the King's household

1372-3 first journey to Italy

1374-86 Controller of Wool Customs

1378 second journey to Italy

c.1387 begins *The Canterbury Tales*

1389 becomes Clerk of the King's Works

1391 moves to Somerset as forester

1399 returns to London

1400 dies at Westminster

An Influential Marriage

About three years after marrying Chaucer, both Philippa and her sister Katherine Swynford were taken on as ladies-in-waiting in John of Gaunt's household. Katherine soon became John's mistress. Some speculate that Philippa did, too, for he often gave her money. But the union between John and Kate was less than casual, for he married her in 1396 – much to the horror of the court. Their great-great-grandson laid claim to the Crown and became Henry VII.

Bodleian Library, Oxford

British Library/E. T. Archive

court, and perhaps he began to copy them then.

In the early 1360s, Chaucer is thought to have withdrawn from court to study for a while, perhaps at Oxford or Cambridge, perhaps at London's Inner Temple. But by 1365, he was back in royal service, and soon to be part of the King's own household.

A document from 22 February 1365 shows him on important diplomatic business in Aquitaine, south-west France, where the alliance between England and the Spanish kingdom of Castile was causing alarm. It seems likely that he was working for the Black Prince, Edward III's eldest son.

Over the next 20 or so years, Chaucer was to make many trips abroad in the King's service, and

Mary Evans Picture Library

Born Londoner
Chaucer's father's house was near the Thames quays where the wine tuns were unloaded. Within a few square miles lived nobility, merchants, beggars, craftsmen, whores, politicians and churchmen: Geoffrey's boyhood was crowded with every class and type. Crown work kept him in touch with London (above) all life long.

Latin education
Geoffrey probably attended, until the age of 12 or 13, a grammar school (left) where the prevailing language was Latin. He was to become a versatile and fluent linguist, translating not just the Latin poets, such as Ovid and Virgil whom he had studied at school, but French and Italian works as well.

it is clear that he was held in high regard and considered capable and discreet. He was also valued as a man of letters and a linguist, well-versed in Italian and the dialects of northern and southern France.

But a yeoman like Chaucer did not only go on important diplomatic missions. He was also expected to make beds, hold torches and serve food at the King's table. He had to entertain the court by telling stories or giving out the latest political news, or with music and songs. Perhaps the young Chaucer now wrote his first verses, romances in the French style. His fellow poet John Gower relates that, 'in the flower of his youth, in various ways', Chaucer filled the country with his 'ditties and glad songs'.

At about the time he entered the King's service, Chaucer married Philippa Roet, a lady-in-waiting to Queen Philippa. The young French poet Froissart wrote of Philippa Chaucer that she had a fine sense of protocol (which she was to need later). The marriage brought Chaucer into closer contact with John of Gaunt, the Duke of Lancaster, Edward's third son and – next to the King – the most powerful man in the kingdom. Philippa became a lady-in-waiting to John's second wife.

Chaucer had known John for some time before Philippa had joined his household, and it was as a memorial to John's first wife, the lovely Blanche who died in 1368, that Chaucer wrote his first major poem, *The Book of the Duchess*.

After the outbreak of the plague that carried off

The Customs man

As Controller of Wool Customs, Chaucer was well placed to know, and make literary use of, the double-dealing that went on in an international port (left) such as London. The Merchant in The Canterbury Tales *is manipulating foreign currency, for instance.*

Hundred Years' War

Begun by Edward III in 1337 as he laid claim to the French throne, the string of major battles and inconclusive skirmishes known as the Hundred Years' War (below) dragged on, draining the economies of Europe and occupying men at a time when Plague had already devastated the population.

Fact or Fiction

BLACK DEATH

In 1348 the Black Death struck. A contemporary wrote, 'This great pestilence . . . raged for a whole year in England so terribly that it cleared many country villages entirely.' On one estimate, more than a third of the population died. It became common to personify Death in art and poetry, and in the Pardoner's Tale three drunks swear that they will seek out and murder the dread Grim Reaper.

Blanche and Edward's Queen Philippa too, the atmosphere at court began to turn sour. The war with France was resumed, disastrously for England. French raids on South Coast ports were frequent, trade was disrupted, and taxes to pay for the war became increasingly burdensome for a population ravaged by the plague. Edward III was slipping into senility, and doted on his rapacious mistress Alice Perrers.

Twice during the 1370s, Chaucer braved the dangers of war to travel to Italy on diplomatic missions, first to Genoa, then to Florence. In Italy he was able to buy copies of poems by the great Italian poets Dante, Petrarch and Boccaccio. He may even have met the latter two. Dante's profound and philosophical work, *Divine Comedy*, proved that poems could encompass a range of ideas and feelings far beyond the scope of the light French court romances. Boccaccio, inspired by the poets of ancient Rome, proclaimed that the poet was not simply an entertainer but also a scholar and philosopher.

COURT CIRCULARS

Chaucer himself became increasingly learned. He collected 'sixty bokes olde and newe' and read voraciously both at home and in London's many libraries, applying both an acute intelligence and scepticism. In this way, he became a highly accomplished scholar, well versed in a variety of subjects from classical literature to the latest scientific and astrological studies of the day.

At the same time, he continued writing poetry in his native language, English – poems achieving a richness far beyond anything in the vernacular

British Library

Mary Evans Picture Library

Peasants' Revolt
The boy-king Richard II was manipulated by rival court factions. He promised mercy to the peasant Wat Tyler and his rebellious followers (left), but later took bloody reprisals, probably on the counsel of his cynical advisors.

Powerful patron
Son of Edward III and uncle of Richard II, John of Gaunt, Duke of Lancaster (below left), was the second most powerful man in England. He sired a dynasty of kings, and was an invaluable patron and contact for Chaucer.

A prized poet
Clearly Chaucer had risen to a position of great status as a poet by the time he was pictured (below) reading a manuscript (probably his narrative poem Troilus and Criseyde) *to the assembled court including Richard and his Queen Anne. Only when plots against the King became rife did Chaucer withdraw to the relative peace of Somerset.*

before. These poems, from *The House of Fame* (c.1374) to *Troilus and Criseyde* (c.1385), were written down and circulated, unlike his early works which were simply recited at court.

All this scholarship and writing occupied him in his spare time, after a long day at work. On 8 June 1374, he was appointed by royal warrant as Controller of the Wool Custom and Wool Subsidy, a very important post, for taxes on exports of wool were the biggest peacetime source of revenue.

The wool taxes were paid to two collectors at the Port of London, and as controller it was Chaucer's job to keep a counter-roll against which the accounts of the collectors could be checked. Before wool was exported, it had to have a licence, sealed by a stamp, one half of which was retained by the controller, and the other by the collectors.

Chaucer was given an apartment, rent-free, above the Aldgate, ten minutes' walk from the Port. But it was not an easy job, for the collectors were often wealthy and powerful merchants with a vested interest in slipping wool through untaxed, and Chaucer was frequently absent on diplomatic missions. Still he remained controller until the end of 1386.

A MYSTERIOUS CASE

These years were, on the whole, prosperous, but his life was not without troubles. A curious document dated 1 May 1380 in the name of Cecily Chaumpaigne releases Geoffrey Chaucer from any action over 'both my rape and other cause'. Could Chaucer have sexually assaulted Mistress Chaumpaigne, or abducted her (which the word 'rape'

Mary Evans Picture Library

The Master and Fellows of Corpus Christi College, Cambridge

also meant then)? One theory is that it was an attempt by London merchants to frame him, but there is no evidence either way.

Whatever the truth there is no doubt that by 1386 he was a man of some substance and status. The year before, he had become a Justice of the Peace and, in October, he entered Parliament as one of the two Knights of the Shire for Kent, where he was now living. But trouble was brewing.

TROUBLE AT COURT

Ever since the death of Edward III in 1377, there had been bitter infighting at court for control of the boy-king Richard II, between the courtiers and aristocrats closest to the boy, the Lancastrians, around John of Gaunt, and the barons. In 1386, the barons gained the upper hand, and began purging the royal household of opponents. A few went to the block and Chaucer, closely associated with both the court party and the Lancastrians, must have felt his position, if not his life, threatened.

Perhaps he was ousted, perhaps he resigned. At all events, he disappeared from royal service for the next few years, and took the chance to begin writing *The Canterbury Tales*.

"God save King Henry, unking'd Richard says"
Hated and envied by many, Richard II was forced to abdicate in favour of Henry Bolingbroke (son of John of Gaunt) at Flint Castle in 1399 (left). He was imprisoned and probably murdered the following year – the same year in which Chaucer himself died. Four months after his coronation, Henry IV renewed Chaucer's annuity of £20 and a barrel of wine, so the poet's last months were comfortable.

Clerk of the Works
Once Richard II was of age, Chaucer found himself in royal favour again. His new post meant that he was wage-master, foreman and administrator, overseeing maintenance (above) of the royal palaces.

Robbed!
Twice in one week Chaucer was set upon by footpads and robbed of wages intended for the building workers (below). What he objected to a great deal more, however, was having his horse stolen each time.

In July 1389, two months after Richard II came of age and began to assert his power, Chaucer was back at work again, this time as Clerk of the Works. This job was, if anything, more arduous than that of controller, for it entailed overseeing the construction and maintenance of many important buildings, such as the Palace of Westminster. In 1390, Chaucer had to organize the restoration of St George's Chapel, Windsor.

As Clerk of the Works, Chaucer had hundreds of men to manage and direct, from master-craftsmen to simple labourers, besides keeping detailed accounts and a check on materials and equipment. It could be dangerous, too: in 1390, Chaucer was attacked and robbed twice in a week.

In 1391 he accepted – perhaps with relief – a job as forester of the King's park in North Petherton,

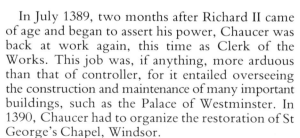

Italian visits
As yeoman in the King's household, Chaucer made frequent trips abroad on business. He spent the winter of 1372-73 in Italy (left) and it is known he went to Florence. Did he meet his contemporary, Petrarch? Or Boccaccio, author of The Decameron *(the so-called 'Italian Canterbury Tales')? Did he acquire, while he was there, books for his great collection? He certainly admired Italian writers, especially Dante, read Italian with ease and spoke it well enough to negotiate loans for Edward III's wars. He returned to Italy in 1378, to Lombardy.*

Somerset. He then had time to continue writing *The Canterbury Tales* – and he was out of the way of the political intrigues building up against the cruel, increasingly tyrannical King Richard.

In February 1399, John of Gaunt died, and Richard, desperate for money to fight wars in France and Ireland, confiscated the Lancastrian estates. Later that year, while Richard was in Ireland, John's son Henry Bolingbroke returned from exile to reclaim his inheritance, and received such ardent support that he soon laid claim to the Crown. Richard was imprisoned, and probably murdered, and Bolingbroke was crowned Henry IV.

Chaucer moved back to London and rented a house in the garden of Westminster Abbey. He seems to have begun to wonder if his poetry was actually a self-indulgence. A text of the time complained that 'demons feed on the songs of the poets, the vanity of worldly wisdom, the pomp of rhetorical language', and Chaucer may have started to feel this was true. At the end of The Parson's Tale, the poet begs forgiveness for his poems, his 'endytinges of worldly vanitee', and describes his regret at writing 'many a song and many a lecherous lay'.

On 25 October 1400, Chaucer died. He was buried in Westminster Abbey, leaving behind him poetry of a richness and depth never before achieved in English, and not to be equalled for 200 years.

Last resting place
Chaucer's last house stood within the grounds of Westminster Abbey (below), and after his death in October 1400 he was buried there – esteemed as a writer, translator and loyal servant of the Crown. It was a rare honour for a commoner, and set a precedent establishing the present 'Poets' Corner'.

THE CANTERBURY TALES

A Prologue introduces us to thirty storytellers drawn from every walk of life, and their shared pilgrimage binds together the varied, dazzling tales they tell one another.

One of the pinnacles of early English literature, *The Canterbury Tales* continues to delight and enthrall readers 600 years after it was penned by Geoffrey Chaucer. The key to the book's greatness lies in its variety. The collection of tales represents not only an exciting and adroit poem, but a compelling drama, an exciting narrative and a remarkably astute assortment of psychological portraits. Through its depiction of a wide range of social types, *The Canterbury Tales* sketches a large-scale canvas of bustling 14th-century English society and also provides an insight into contemporary attitudes towards such diverse subjects as Church, marriage, materialism and the role of women.

GUIDE TO THE PLOT

The structure of *The Canterbury Tales* is a simple one. In a prologue that introduces the main characters, Chaucer tells us of 29 pilgrims who are gathered at the Tabard Inn in Southwark on their way to visit the shrine of St Thomas à Becket in Canterbury. Deciding to accompany them, the innkeeper proposes that, to pass the time on the pilgrimage, each of them should tell four stories, two on the outward journey and two on the way back, and "who tells upon the road / Tales of best sense, in most amusing mode, / Shall have a supper at the others' cost."

Although Chaucer never fulfilled this grand scheme – he finished only 22 of the tales and did not complete all the linking conversations – he did succeed in giving an impression of comprehensiveness and unity. The Miller's Tale is a rude burlesque of the Knight's, and the Oxford Clerk's Tale seems in part a reply to the Wife of Bath. Themes of love, marriage and religion tie the stories together.

The tales reflect a good deal of Chaucer's own attitudes and preoccupations. His hostility to Church corruption is evident in his stinging portrayals of the Pardoner and the Friar, who contrast so markedly with the simple goodness of the Parson; and the increasing avarice of the age is revealed in the Merchant, the Sailor, the Pardoner and the Physician.

Perhaps the major theme is the nature, role and constancy of Woman, a thread that runs right through the tales. The Knight and the Clerk discuss an idealized image of womanhood, while the Miller

The Tabard Inn
It is at a London inn (above) that the narrator, Chaucer, falls into company with 29 motley pilgrims. The innkeeper decides to join them on their journey to Canterbury and suggests the perfect entertainment for the tedious, arduous trip.

The Prologue
In the lengthy introduction we meet the assorted pilgrims with Chaucer and the Host in among them (below). The descriptions of physical appearance and character are often laced with sharp wit and irony. It is Chaucer's way to damn with faint praise, to detract with a flick of the pen. The pilgrims' tales are interlinked by passages of dialogue in which they quarrel, criticize each other's efforts at storytelling, and discuss social issues.

> "In Southwark, at the Tabard, as I lay
> Ready to start upon my pilgrimage
> To Canterbury, full of devout homage,
> There came at nightfall to that hostelry
> Some nine and twenty in a company
> Of sundry persons who had chanced to fall
> In fellowship, and pilgrims were they all."

Walter's chosen bride

Urged to take a wife and produce an heir, the Marquis of Lombardy chooses a girl he has seen while out hunting (left) – the daughter of a poor woodsman. She is asked to swear perfect obedience, then she is stripped of her rags and dressed in finery.

the Marquis resolves to test Griselda's steadfastness. On the pretext that the noblemen are troubled by her lowly birth, he arranges for a bodyguard to take away their daughter. Of Griselda it is said: "meek as a lamb, she sat there, still, / And let this cruel sergeant do his will." She thinks the baby is to be killed: in fact, it is taken to be brought up as a noblewoman by the Marquis' sister in Bologna.

Some years later, the Marquis does the same with their son, and again Griselda accepts his decision without objection. The final test comes when Walter seemingly makes arrangements to renounce his marriage and take a new wife, and insists that Griselda returns to her lowly life with her father.

Taken on a realistic level, The Clerk's is

and the Merchant offer portraits that are bawdier and more bitter. It is the Wife of Bath who comes centre-stage to voice Woman's own earthy, realistic viewpoint.

Chaucer is a magnificent storyteller and creator of character, but an equally striking feature of *The Canterbury Tales* is his complete mastery of a wide range of literary forms. He slips from sermon to satire with complete ease and appears equally at home dealing with courtly romance, rude farce or beast fable. The following three tales are representative of the work's scope and achievement – its stylistic variety, structural ingenuity and complexity of character. Through the vitality of his language and imagination, Chaucer brings a medieval world teeming with life into our modern consciousness.

THE CLERK'S TALE

As befits his serious demeanour, the Clerk tells a moral tale which he "learned once, at Padua, of a worthy clerk", the clerk being the 14th-century Italian writer Petrarch. A youthful, impetuous Marquis in Lombardy, Walter, is exhorted by his people to settle down and take a wife. Somewhat reluctantly, he agrees and chooses a beautiful peasant girl, Griselda, whom he has seen while hunting. His proposal to her hints at the trials to come: "I'd ask her if her will it be / To be my wife and so be ruled by me . . ."

After some years of marriage, "it happened, as it has sometimes before", that

More than patient

Modern readers find it hard to swallow when a woman meekly permits the 'murder' of her children (right). To appreciate the original by Petrarch, the story has to be read with the eyes of a medieval Italian. But Chaucer does invite critical judgement – about the nature of marriage and power.

Victor Ambrus © 1985 from *Canterbury Tales* (McCaughrean) published by O.U.P.

Bodleian Library, Oxford

Barrel of laughs

John the Carpenter, already guilty of the folly of marrying a young wife, commits the grosser foolishness of trusting her in the company of the 'intellectual' lodger, Nicholas (below left). When Nicholas says that the angels have revealed to him the coming of the Second Flood, John is all too willing to follow instructions and hang in an improvised 'ark' from the rafters (left), waiting to ride out the Inundation.

THE MILLER'S TALE

In complete contrast is the tale recounted by the Miller; a classic *fabliau* – the term used for a medieval short story about lower-class characters and intrigue, including saucy and salacious material. In this case the young wife of a carpenter, Alison, is desired by their lodger, an astrologer, Nicholas, and also by a prim parish clerk, Absalom. Absalom takes to serenading her by guitar but "she was

Cock-and-fox story

The farmyard setting of the Nun's Priest's Tale is as commonplace as possible (below). But the language and imagery climb to an altogether higher plane, the cock resembling a chivalric monarch troubled by omens. The rhetoric collapses as the action degenerates into a knockabout chase (right).

enamoured so of Nicholas/That Absalom might go and blow his horn".

She and Nicholas plan a trick on her husband, John, so that they can spend the night together. John trusts his lodger completely, so Nicholas informs John that his astrological charts are predicting an imminent flood and that he must hang three separate tubs up among the roof beams for each of them "Wherein we may swim out as in a barge,/And have therein sufficient food and drink" until the water subsides. The carpenter obediently does so, and when he falls asleep in his tub, Nicholas and Alison slip out of theirs and retire to bed together.

However, Absalom takes it into his head to call at Alison's window that night. From this point onwards, the farcical events become more lewd, as Absalom suffers vulgar humiliations, Nicholas deservedly gets a scalded backside as payment for breaking wind in Absalom's face and the credulous carpenter, mistaking all the noise and confusion for a Second Flood, cuts free his tub and hurtles down the roof. It is an indelicate tale, recounted by the Miller with drunken, exuberant gusto, and typifying his coarse, lively personality.

Bodleian Library, Oxford

an uncomfortable tale, with Griselda presented as an unappealing symbol of subjection and Walter inhumanly cruel. This was not the Clerk's intention:

"This story's told here, not that all wives should/ Follow Griselda in humility,/ For this would be unbearable, though they would,/ But just that everyone, in his degree,/ Should be as constant in adversity."

Nevertheless the tale is given additional interest and tension by the fact that it has some disturbing things to say about social and sexual relations of the time – the relation between Walter and Griselda being an allegory both of the cruelty of the governing towards the governed, and of masculine dominance. The Clerk's outlook is more than counteracted, however, by the presence of the Wife of Bath, a pilgrim who has determinedly made her way through no fewer than five husbands. Griselda represents her antithesis – obedient rather than domineering, patient and serene rather than nagging and overbearing. The Clerk's Tale makes for compelling narrative, but we are left in no doubt as to which kind of woman Chaucer prefers.

SAINT THOMAS À BECKET

In 1162 Becket was made Archbishop of Canterbury by his close friend Henry II, who thought to use Thomas as his 'inside man' within the Church. But Becket became a devout churchman and thwarted Henry. He was murdered in Canterbury Cathedral in 1170 by the King's knights. The crime and Becket's courage became legendary. The King did penance at his tomb and Becket was canonized. His shrine quickly acquired a reputation for miraculous cures, and pilgrims flocked to it.

THE NUN'S PRIEST'S TALE
Quite different from the other stories, The Nun's Priest's Tale takes the form of an animal fable. The hero is a cock called Chanticleer, who loves the hen Pertelote; together they sing in perfect harmony.

However, when Chanticleer has a bad dream about a beast in the barnyard who has come to kill him, Pertelote is outraged by his faint-heartedness, and they exchange lofty philosophical and mythological references about the prophetic accuracy – or otherwise – of dreams. Ultimately accepting his love's advice and reassurance, Chanticleer disregards his dream and flies down from his beam into the yard.

However, one day the cock is alarmed to see a fox approaching. "The cause of my coming/Was only just to listen to you sing", says the fox disarmingly. While Chanticleer is basking in the flattery, the fox seizes the cock and runs off, with rescuers in hot pursuit. In his triumph the fox should know when to keep his mouth shut; for when Chanticleer gets him to speak, the cock is able to break free from

first by his beloved and then by the fox's flattery, and he nearly pays a heavy price for it. For the fox, the moral is: "God give him mischance / Who is so indiscreet in governance / He chatters when he ought to hold his peace."

In some ways, however, this tale is ridiculing the whole notion of a moral. The story's charm lies in the way it is told. It is an exercise in the 'mock heroic' – a spoof on rhetorical epic poetry in the grand vein. Here a cock and hen are improbably endowed not only with speech but with a sophisticated knowledge of dreams, medicine, philosophy and courtly love. Their argument deliciously sends up not only medieval rhetoric, but also the intellectual pretensions of the day. Yet far from seeming like a writer's joke peculiar to its time, the tale remains one of the most universal and modern in appeal.

"... like one mad he started in to cry,
'Help! Water! Water! Help! For God's dear heart!'
This carpenter out of his sleep did start,
Hearing that 'Water!' cried as madman would,
And thought, 'Alas, now comes down Noel's flood!'"

Journey's end
The pilgrims arrive at Canterbury (below) and all secular thoughts of storytelling are laid aside in favour of the true purpose of their pilgrimage.

the fox's open mouth and to fly to safety.

For the cock, the moral is: "He who shuts his eyes when he should see, / And wilfully, God let him ne'er be free!" He has allowed his judgement to be swayed,

CHARACTERS IN FOCUS

The Prologue to *The Canterbury Tales* introduces a cavalcade of characters, whose physical characteristics denote personality – as do Chaucer's wry comments.

WHO'S WHO

The Host   Innkeeper of the Tabard Inn at Southwark who proposes each pilgrim tells tales to enliven the journey.

The Merchant   Secretly in debt and involved in illegal currency deals, he does business in a "stately way", wearing a "Flemish beaver hat".

The Wife of Bath   A big, ruddy nagging widow, deaf in one ear. She has been on pilgrimages before, perhaps in search of husbands, and has been married five times.

The Knight   "A true and perfect gentle knight" who has fought in the Crusades. The Squire's father.

Chaucer   represents himself as a shy, talentless poet; his contribution to the competition is cut short by his exasperated audience.

The Monk   As inspector of his master's estates, he has ample chance to indulge his passion for hunting and elaborately fine dress.

The Friar   A mendicant (beggar-monk) who fawns on the rich but despises the poor: "there is no profit in dealing with [them]".

The Prioress   Head of a convent, accompanied by a nun and three priests, she is vain, affected and coy.

The Cook   A drunken, insanitary servant of the guildsmen, who has the annoying habit of picking at a sore on his leg.

The Pardoner   Purveyor of papal indulgences and bogus holy relics, he is a man full of false flattery and confidence tricks.

The Parson   A parish priest of utmost integrity, fitted "to draw folk to heaven by fair behaviour and good example".

The Sailor   "no man from Hull to Carthage" knows more about the sea. But he carries a hidden dagger and admits to a little piracy here and there.

The Summoner   Empowered to summon wrongdoers to appear before ecclesiastical courts, his abuse of power and corrupt character are physically manifested in his repulsive, leprous skin.

THE CLERK OF OXENFORD'S TALE

A student of philosophy and of the priesthood, the Clerk (below) is shabbily dressed and mounted on a scrawny, ill-fed horse, because he spends all his money on books. "You ride as shy and silent as a maid who's newly married", says the Host accusingly, and we are told elsewhere that the Clerk "never spoke a word more than necessary". He gives the impression of being an unworldly figure completely absorbed in his studies – even to the exclusion of participating in real life. His tale about the patient Griselda has dual implications for his character: its moral overtones reflect his sobriety, and the fact that the tale is borrowed from the works of the Italian poet Petrarch reinforces our image of the man as a scholar.

Walter and Griselda enjoy a strange marriage (left). The behaviour of this Italian Marquis is excused so often that we quickly suspect Chaucer's sympathies do not lie there. With masculine insensitivity, he can only convince himself of Griselda's obedience by setting increasingly inhuman tests for her. In the course of the story he tends to become simply an instrument with which the fortitude of a Christian soul is put to the trial. Griselda is essentially a two-dimensional model of marital loyalty and Christian forbearance. "When it comes to virtue and beauty, then there was none more fair beneath the sun." Yet modern readers do not like her. She speaks with the voice of a peasant, too – a peasant accustomed to the brutality of the ruling class. "I never thought I merited at all to be your wife, nor yet your servant-girl." She is talking of 'merit' in social terms: in moral terms she is clearly her husband's superior. The Wife of Bath has a very different picture of marriage to portray.

THE MILLER'S TALE

THE NUN'S PRIEST'S TALE

The Priest known to the rest as 'Sir John', (right) is invited by the Host to do better than the dull and droning Monk whose shapeless story has been irritating and boring the pilgrims. This storyteller is sometimes referred to as the 'faceless pilgrim', as there is no description of him, even in the Prologue. His character is implied only by the nature of the tale – a delightful, clever parody of medieval rhetoric and philosophy. At the end he invites his listeners to make what they like of it, taking to heart the "morality", with or without "the chaff". The Tale has plenty of "chaff" – comic digressions, burlesque, knock-about humour and a bit of ribaldry besides.

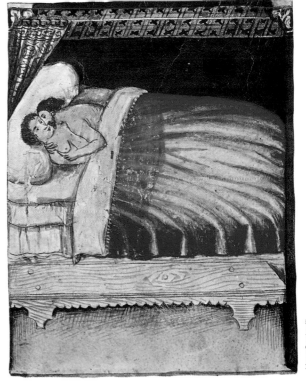

Mary Evans Picture Library

Chanticleer and Pertelote (above) live on an exalted, chivalric plain concerning themselves with the significance of dreams, the motion of the stars, the classics, philosophy . . . purgatives and sex. They swoop from the sublime to the banal. Pertelote "truly held the heart of Chanticleer bound and captive". So he who has "no equal in crowing" but who is somewhat given to vanity allows himself to be undermined by a cajoling woman.

The Miller is a champion wrestler capable of knocking down a door with his head (below). He is "a thick set knave" with a red beard and "mouth as wide as a great furnace" – coarse, violent, ribald and argumentative. His bawdy tale is in keeping with his vulgarity, and he insists on telling it as soon as the Knight finishes his. In his drunken state, perhaps he thinks to emulate the Knight's chivalric romance. His tale is also about two rival suitors to the same woman, but the Miller's 'heroes' have quite different sexual aspirations from those of the Knight.

Alison has many admirers, but only Nicholas wins the privilege of cuckolding her husband (right). Nicholas is a "sweet clerk" who dabbles in astrology. His speech is courtly enough, but his actions are vulgar. He is eminently civil to his "beloved and esteemed host", but only in order to make a fool of him. The repeated use of "pleasant" is ironic. Alison could be a highly unsympathetic character, but her sexual amorality is compared to that of "a colt" and "a barn swallow", and her promiscuity becomes nothing more than an absorption in the world of instinct and pleasure. Her husband is the fool.

Mauro Pucciarelli

19

PAGEANT OF LIFE

Chaucer was constrained by the tastes of his patrons and the conventions of the time; but over the years he brought something very new, very English to the arts of poetry and storytelling.

or a busy civil servant, Geoffrey Chaucer managed to write a remarkable quantity of verse, improving as he matured. He composed five substantial poems – *The Book of the Duchess, The House of Fame, The Parliament of Fowls, The Legend of Good Women,* the very long and leisurely *Troilus and Criseyde* (often described as a novel in verse) – as well as his crowning masterpiece, *The Canterbury Tales.* He also wrote a number of short poems and translated several works from French and Latin, both poetic and scholarly.

ENIGMATIC AUTHOR

We learn little of the man himself from Chaucer's works. Any character of his that might be identified with the poet is treated with a mocking condescension: the narrator of *The Parliament of Fowls* knows nothing of his principal subject, love, and the poet in *The Canterbury Tales* is a tongue-tied creature who tells a tale (*Sir Thopas*) that parodies bad popular romances. In fact it is more than likely that Chaucer, a seasoned man of affairs, was the complete opposite of the *Canterbury Tales* poet in appearance as well as behaviour, and that the 'self-portraits' are jokes contemporary audiences could appreciate.

Chaucer's readers would have been a small group, mainly consisting of people in or around court circles who would all have known one another. The English court was a sophisticated, cultural place at the time, with a literary tradition that was overwhelmingly French, since the language was still widely spoken among the English upper class, and the superiority of French poetry was unquestioned. Chaucer seems to have begun his literary career by translating the most famous of all medieval poems, *The Romance of the Rose.* Early poems such as *The Book of the Duchess* owe a great deal to French literary forms, but later he was also influenced by contemporary Italian writers such as Dante, Boccaccio and Petrarch. From the beginning Chaucer manipulated his sources skilfully, and by the 1380s, when he wrote *The Parliament of Fowls, Troilus and Criseyde* and *The Canterbury Tales,* he had absorbed them completely and found his own distinctive voice.

Although he was undoubtedly the greatest writer of his time, Chaucer was also fortunate in his court background and Continental culture. Other outstanding poems of the period, for example William Langland's *Vision of Piers Plowman* and the anonymous *Sir Gawain and the Green Knight,* happened to be written in the 'wrong' dialect and in unrhymed early English verse-forms that were soon to be abandoned. The result is that they are today (and have long been) difficult for most people other than specialized scholars. Chaucer wrote in the dialect of the south-

Henry Holiday: Dante and Beatrice/National Museums and Galleries on Merseyside, Walker Art Gallery, Liverpool

Dante and Beatrice
Chaucer was profoundly influenced by the works of the great Italian poet Dante and, above all, by his monumental Divine Comedy, *a poem inspired by his unrequited love for Beatrice Portinari (left).*

Italian master
Chaucer's Clerk's Tale *is based on a story by the great Italian poet Petrarch (above), whom he may have met in 1373.*

The Romance of the Rose

The most famous of all medieval courtly romances (above), the Roman de la Rose, *was translated by Chaucer into English. It tells of a poet who dreams of a garden where he is struck by love, but he must overcome many problems to fulfill his desire.*

Boccaccio

Chaucer borrowed many ideas from this Italian poet (left, centre). Il Filostrato – *a tale of lust – became, in Chaucer's* Troilus and Criseyde, *a deeply moving poem about truth in love.*

east – the direct ancestor of modern English – using rhyming verse-forms, based on Continental ones, that became the staple elements in English poetry for centuries to come. That is why his verse can be 'translated' into modern English in a form that remains reasonably close to the original, and even the original can be tackled with a little effort. The dialect of the court, the City and the universities were to become 'standard English' in time; and Chaucer's work gave the language stature, making it a medium as respectable as French for ambitious literary endeavours. Chaucer was also a great innovator and enriched the language with many words and phrases, seen for the first time in his work.

Most of the words in Chaucer's originals are still part of English today, although they may not always be recognizable. Sometimes the spelling may be very different – the "sweet showers" in the opening line of a translation of *The Prologue*, for instance, were Chaucer's 'shoures soote'. Chaucer's English is basically the same language as modern English, but it actually sounded quite different. Vowels in particular were given a much fuller sound, and many words ended in a soft, almost silent vowel – Chaucer pronounced 'name' as in Viet'nam'. Yet often the meaning becomes clear as soon as the poems are read aloud – as indeed they should be, for they were written to be read to an audience as much as in private. Only then can the wonderful fluting

sound of the language which Chaucer created be fully appreciated.

Much of Chaucer's work follows medieval conventions, notably in his use of the dream, allegory and courtly love. But *The Parliament of Fowls* shows his characteristically humorous and subversive way of treating them; the lower orders among the birds not only criticize the conventions of courtly love but also win their mates, whereas the noble eagles, entangled in their high-flown code, must wait a year for a decision.

Chaucer's scribes
Living before the age of printing, Chaucer employed scribes to copy his poems by hand. In one poem, Chaucer rages against 'Adam' for a certain 'negligence and rape' in transcribing his work. But after his death, Chaucer's poems could be read and enjoyed in lovely illuminated manuscripts (far left).

Other medieval writers were of course aware of the conflicts between the real and the ideal, the courtly and the carnal; but Chaucer is unique in his ability to operate on both planes at the same time. *Troilus and Criseyde* is a story of high romance in the accepted style, but then the practical realism of Pandarus intervenes to get the lovers into bed together. And whereas tradition portrayed Criseyde as a stereotyped 'faithless woman', Chaucer presents her more sympathetically. Finally, in *The Canterbury Tales*, Chaucer revealed his full originality. He created a series of individual portraits drawn from all classes of society – something that had never been done before in English, let alone with the poet's sly, tolerant humour. And he transformed a standard structure – the collection of stories within a 'frame' situation – into something new in medieval literature; for the story-outside-the-stories moves towards a destination while its characters chatter, chaff, row and come to blows.

Chaucer's reputation dominated 15th-century English literature. William Caxton, who introduced printing into England, thought that it was not worth publishing any book in English earlier than *The Canterbury Tales*, the prime work of the man who 'embellished, ornated and made fair our English'.

Love's story
The unifying theme of The Canterbury Tales *is Love and the battle of the sexes (right). Literature in general was much given over to the courtly arts of wooing, but Chaucer brought to the subject a new realism and gusto, as he explored the forces of chivalry, lust, infatuation, marriage, abuse of power, jealousy, temptation, cuckoldry . . .*

Greatly influenced by the classical and European literature available to him, Chaucer wrote within a literary tradition for most of his life. He was poet, song-writer and translator *par excellence*.

But with the passage of time, he experimented, and his work took on an individualistic verve and originality. *The Parliament of Fowls* (c.1380-82) is a wry parody of chivalric conventions, as well as an ambitious analysis of the nature of Love. *Troilus and Criseyde* (c.1382-85) was based on a story already known to his audience. But in his unhurried narrative, where the tragic action grows out of the characters of the participants, he brought a humane, compassionate attitude to his writing which makes interesting reading, even now.

These are not Chaucer's only works by any means, but the only ones, besides his masterpiece, *The Canterbury Tales* (1387-1400) – in which all his skills reached their supreme expression – which still reward a modern reader.

THE PARLIAMENT OF FOWLS

→ c.1380-82 ←

The regal eagles (right) are devoted to the chivalric code in Chaucer's delightful allegorical poem about the nature of Love. With typical self-mockery, Chaucer makes the narrator a naive figure who 'knows not love in deed', but has often read about it in books. After reading an old text, the poet dreams that one of the characters in the book leads him to the gates of a wonderful garden, on which are written two intriguing sentences: 'This is the way to all good fortune' and 'Abstinence is the only remedy'. Inside the park, where the weather is always perfect and no-one is sick or old, the dreamer sees a temple to Venus, goddess of Love, inside which are sad paintings with stories of lust and betrayal. Looking for solace, the narrator spies a lovely glade where Nature presides over a turbulent conference. It is St Valentine's Day, when all the birds assemble to choose their mates. Each bird takes its place, the birds of prey supreme, small worm-eating birds in the middle, waterfowl at the bottom, with seed-eating birds filling the grass between. Three eagles vie lengthily for the love of the same lady eagle – so lengthily that the lower birds interrupt. A raucous parliamentary debate ensues in which they deride the eagles' code of courtly love. Finally, the poet wakes, none the wiser, and vows to go on . . . reading.

Edward Burne-Jones: *Parlement of Foules/Fotomas*

TROILUS AND CRISEYDE

→ c.1382-85 ←

The noble prince Troilus and his lady love Criseyde (left) are hero and heroine of this long, moving narrative poem. It is an old story about a tragic love affair in the times of the Trojan War. But in Chaucer's poem, Troilus is a knight in armour, Troy a bustling city. Troilus, son of the Trojan King whose city is besieged by the Greeks, languishes with love for Criseyde. This lovely young widow has managed to live down the shameful defection of her father, Calkas, to the Greeks.

Troilus confides his love to Pandarus who offers to act as go-between. Criseyde is persuaded to accept Troilus as her sworn knight, and eventually to allow him into her bed. Their bliss is interrupted when Calkas (now in the Greek camp) arranges an exchange of prisoners to win back the company of his daughter. Vowing to return, the heart-broken Criseyde is forced to leave Troy, escorted by the handsome Greek warrior Diomede. Soon, however, her letters to Troilus alter in tone, and the distraught lover begins to suspect that Criseyde has broken her solemn vows of love and given herself to another knight.

British Library/Bridgeman Art Library

annual income was £875 at a time when one was thought well off on £5 a year.

English society in Chaucer's day, although passionately religious, was almost as fervently anti-clerical. As people began to understand more of the Gospel, so they began to judge the clerics by the standards they taught. And some did not stand up to close inspection. As Langland put it in his poem *Piers Plowman*: 'Covetousness has overcome the priests and all clergy/And the unlettered are led (unless our Lord helps them)/By such incompetent clergy to incurable agonies.' The English Church in the 14th century no longer demanded the rejection of all worldly goods. The great monastic houses had become (as shown in Chaucer's fictional Monk and Prioress) comfortable places for well-born but landless men and women. Thus the hunting monk became a common target of criticism. He was not perceived as wicked, but people objected to his lifestyle which was remarkably similar to that of the landed gentry rather than being governed by monastic rule.

And the friars (monks dependent on charity), who had found their special niche in schools and universities, invited criticism for chasing wealthy patronage: 'Friars follow after rich folk/And put little price upon poor people.'

Officers of the Church were empowered to

An increasingly common feature of 14th-century church life was the chantry, an endowment by a wealthy patron for the saying of daily masses for his soul and the souls of his family. The chantries could be comfortable sinecures which left a cleric plenty of time free to curry favour with rich patrons and 'drum up' further trade. Especially in London, where many of the wealthiest people in the country congregated, this could be highly lucrative. The clamour of bells was to be heard there every morning, signifying the celebration of masses – a sort of 14th-century status symbol.

PROFESSIONAL CONNECTIONS

The Church not only served the rich, it also helped to *make* men rich. In medieval England, it offered the one real chance of rising above the social class of one's birth. The disadvantage of humble beginnings could be flung off by studying at one of the church schools and progressing to Oxford or Cambridge. All students were in minor holy orders and most proceeded to the priesthood. A trained clerk might become an estate manager for some great monastery or for a nobleman. The Law recruited solely from among university students. And of course the Civil Services of both the royal court and the papal administration were staffed by trained priests. Once a successful young student found himself a rich patron, humble birth was no bar to advancement. The richest Englishman of his time, William of Wykeham, who was King Edward III's Chancellor (1367-1371) and Bishop of Winchester, was the son of a 'villein' – that is, a farm worker tied to the land of his overlord. And William of Wykeham's

Divine retribution
The Black Death was looked upon as a punishment visited on Mankind by God (above), and increased the sense of need for strict religious observance of and obedience to God's laws.

Sin personified
Sin and temptation took on a very vivid reality by being portrayed as imps and demons (right).

Monkish mischief
A more educated laity began to expect higher standards of behaviour from their clergy. The 'weaknesses' and shortcomings of those in holy orders (left) started to invite censure.

Treasures in heaven
Indulgences were granted by a pardoner (right) to 'exempt' people from time in Purgatory. It was a system that could be, and was, easily abused.

grant indulgences – dispensations from the Pope allowing 'days off' torment in Purgatory. The sale of such indulgences for money was a growing practice; and although originally not intended as a swindle, it was fast becoming exactly that: a cynical exploitation of people's fear. And the Pope did little to stamp it out. The Pardoner in *The Canterbury Tales* claims he can absolve sin completely with his indulgences. He also carries phoney relics – supposed possessions or bodily remains of the saints – promising blessings to those who paid to touch them. It is easy to understand why such shameless confidence tricksters should incense men like Chaucer who saw rogues in clerical garb taking advantage of the ignorant and frightened.

Absentee priests drew salaries from parishes they never visited; chantry priests fawned on rich patrons who would ensure rich livings for their friends and families; bishops were obliged to toady to both King and Pope. Yet despite these abuses and corruptions, it would be wrong to assume that

Cult of the Virgin

Hail Mary full of wynne [grace]/The Holy Ghost is thee within/Blessed be thou over all women/And be the fruit of thy womb. Amen.

There was a very great emphasis placed on the role of the Virgin Mary (above) as intercessor for sinners. The downfall of Man was blamed on Eve; but salvation was possible through the second Eve – the mother of Jesus.

John Wyclif

The famed radical theologian Wyclif (above right) instigated the first translation of the Bible into the language of the people. And when he argued against the extent of papal taxes (from the cloistered seclusion of Oxford University), his arguments suited the King's purposes. Later Wyclif became more extreme, less 'acceptable' – and was consequently shunned.

the whole spiritual fabric of the kingdom was rotten. The records teem with intelligent, conscientious ministers who were witty, perceptive, lively and well-informed. Richard Rolle, a mystic hermit who preached abstinence, meditation, prayer and spirituality by his own example, and the visionary Mother Julian were just two such examples. Capable and educated ministers challenged the less educated in matters of faith. Humble parsons, like the one in *The Canterbury Tales*, whose ministry is unobtrusive and selfless, were equally typical.

The loudest critics of the favoured few were often those trained priests who had *not* managed to attract the favour of a patron or were perhaps saddled with a wretchedly paid curacy for an absentee rector. William Langland, for example, most virulent of critics, was himself a clerk in minor orders,

27

denying the Pope's right to tax the Church, and he was certainly not making a bid to free England from the grip of Rome. Wyclif's scholarly arguments and refutations were wagged at the Pope only until rival claimants to the papal throne were rendering the papacy too weak to oppose the English king. Once the challenge had gone out of the 'game', the propaganda campaign was dropped, and as Wyclif's ideas became more and more extreme, he was abandoned by his noble patrons. Only the wildest of his followers, though, went as far as to reject papal authority altogether, and preached Christian socialism. Independent of Wyclif, John Ball preached a classless society. He was imprisoned and excommunicated, but freed from gaol by the mob during the Peasants' Revolt. He urged the execution of all lords, prelates and monks, but was hanged after the defeat of the uprising. His efforts had only served (by unjust association) to discredit John Wyclif with the landed classes, and many more besides.

Despite the dissent and the abuses of the time, it was a pious, believing age. Chaucer's pilgrims are as varied a collection of saints and sinners as could be found: yet they all devote time and money to travel to Canterbury to honour the most famous English saint of the time. They would all have seen themselves as members of the all-pervasive Church. All education, literacy, law and managerial skills stemmed from it. The Church provided for the care of each individual soul throughout life and after. Although flawed in practice, it was a Church which no-one would have been able to ignore.

who failed to rise through the Church's hierarchy.

Some have seen a similar bitterness and envy at the root of John Wyclif's radical theology. John Wyclif spent most of his life at Oxford University, and his theological discussions were conducted in Latin along traditional lines. But he fervently believed that Christians should be able to hear and read the Bible in everyday English. He translated the New Testament himself – the whole Bible was ready by 1388. He attacked the growing secular power of the Pope and condemned the priesthood for trying to monopolize Christ's mercy.

Wyclif enjoyed the patronage of John of Gaunt, the third son of Edward III, and proved a useful tool to Edward III. As early as 1343, Edward encouraged Parliament to write to the Pope and protest against his demands for revenue from the English Church. This was just one tactical move in Edward's game-like political struggle with the Pope. He had no intention of

The pilgrim way
Pilgrimages (above) were a popular religious observance of the time. And the most important saint of all in the 14th century, to English pilgrims, was Thomas à Becket, whose shrine stood in Canterbury Cathedral.

Hellfire and mercy
Because so much art survives showing souls in torment (left), Hell, demons and the Devil, it is widely assumed that the laity of the Middle Ages cowered in fear of the after-life, their anxieties fuelled by a cynical, power-hungry clergy. But there is just as much proof of a caring, tender, merciful religion portraying a Saviour (right) extending a democratic redemption towards rich and poor, serf and nobleman alike.

WILLIAM SHAKESPEARE

◆ 1564 - 1616 ◆

Much is known about Shakespeare, the public figure: that he
enjoyed a meteoric rise in the world of theatre; that he became
a rich man, and that he retired – somewhat mysteriously – to
Stratford while still at the height of his powers. We know very
little, however, about the private man, and can only speculate
on whom he loved; whom he addressed in his hauntingly
beautiful sonnets; what he felt when writing the world's 'best
for Comedy and Tragedy'.

Myths and Follies

Shakespeare has inspired a huge amount of biographical research, but wild speculation has often taken over from sober interpretation, leading to outlandish fantasies about his life and work.

It is often said that little is known of Shakespeare's life, but the assertion is only partly true. For a man of his time, in his profession, the amount of solid information that has survived about Shakespeare is fairly substantial. Most, however, is contained in colourless official documents (baptismal records, papers relating to the sale of property, and so on) – sources that tell us nothing about the man's personality.

Biographers have naturally been keen to flesh out the figure of Shakespeare, drawing on local traditions about him and also on inferences about his life or personality contained in his work, but these practices are fraught with difficulty. Certainly Shakespeare sometimes alluded to contemporary events, and it is often tempting to connect passages in his work to his own life (for example Prospero's beautiful final speeches in *The Tempest*, which sound like the author's farewell to the stage). But Shakespeare's writing is so many-sided that this kind of link can never be more than intriguing speculation.

THE BACONIAN HERETICS

Some admirers of Shakespeare's works, however, have been so unsatisfied with the prosaic biographical outlines, that they have come to the wayward conclusion that the lad from Stratford cannot have grown into one of the world's greatest writers, and that someone else must have penned the immortal works for him. The evidence that Shakespeare did in fact write the plays and poems that bear his name is so abundant, unambiguous, consistent and cogent that it seems astonishing that any rational person could doubt it, but the arguments of the 'anti-Stratfordians' have more to do with snobbery and misplaced imagination than with common sense.

As far as is known, nobody seriously doubted the orthodox opinion – that Shakespeare wrote Shakespeare – until the late 18th century, and it was not until the mid-19th century that a movement to discredit Shakespeare began. The book that started it off was written by an American

Many-sided genius
Philosopher, statesman and essayist, Francis Bacon (right) was one of the intellectual giants of his age. Some misguided admirers think he was also the true author of the plays bearing Shakespeare's name (inset).

called Joseph C. Hart and bore the unlikely title of *The Romance of Yachting* (1848). His ideas were taken up by his fellow countrywoman Delia Bacon, who was convinced that her namesake Francis Bacon, one of the most eminent public figures of Shakespeare's day, was the mastermind behind the plays, directing a group of authors to express his ideas.

Miss Bacon thought that the 'Stratford poacher' was a 'vulgar, illiterate man', a member of a 'dirty, doggish group of players', and therefore could not have written the great works attributed to him. She died insane in 1859, but her work was carried on by a host of followers, maintaining her line that the author of the supreme masterpieces of English literature must be a highly educated, cultured man, not a country bumpkin.

The 'proof' of these sceptics consisted mainly in pointing out verbal correspondences (most of them so commonplace as to be inconsequential) between the works that went under the name of Shakespeare and the undoubted works of Bacon, and in finding concealed 'messages' in these writings. The height of absurdity was reached in 1910 when one of the most distinguished of all Baconians, Sir Edwin Durning-Lawrence, published *Bacon is Shakespeare*. In this book, Sir Edwin –

Digging for the truth
In 1909 Orville Ward Owen, a Detroit physician and dedicated Baconian, thought he had decoded a message revealing that manuscripts were buried near the River Wye which would prove that Bacon wrote Shakespeare. He excavated for years (above), but found nothing.

otherwise a sane man – claimed to have discovered a coded message in the First Folio edition of Shakespeare's works (1623) which proved not only that Bacon wrote it, but also that he intended this message to be unveiled in 1910, the very year in which *Bacon is Shakespeare* was published.

Professional code-breakers have shown that using Baconian methods one can find virtually any message one wants to find in virtually any book,

and other Baconian 'evidence' is just as worthless. Nevertheless, the Baconians still keep going, and they are not the only 'disbelievers', for there is now a host of other 'claimants'. Chief among them is Edward de Vere, 17th Earl of Oxford, a courtier, literary patron and amateur poet. His claims were first put forward by a Gateshead schoolteacher called J. Thomas Looney in a book published in 1920 (recognizing that the author's name would be a gift to sarcastic reviewers the publishers tried to persuade Looney to adopt a pseudonym, but he bravely resisted).

MESSAGES FROM THE SPIRIT WORLD
One of Looney's followers in the Oxfordian camp, Percy Allen, had the bright idea of engaging a medium 'of unimpeachable integrity' through whom he talked to Shakespeare, Bacon and Oxford. Their heavenly testimony, recorded in *Talks with Elizabethans* (1947), was that the plays were works of collaboration, with Oxford the major contributor. Even without the support of messages from beyond the grave, Oxford is a slightly more plausible claimant than Bacon, but an objection that none of his supporters has been able to get round is that he died in 1604, when several of Shakespeare's most celebrated plays were still to be written.

Other candidates (of varying degrees of absurdity) who have been put forward as claimants to Shakespeare's laurels include the actor Richard Burbage, assorted poets and playwrights of the period – including Ben Jonson, Christopher Marlowe and Edmund Spenser – a team of Jesuits, Elizabeth I and Mary Queen of Scots.

Apart from the authorship question, the lunatic fringe has been more often attracted to the sonnets than to any other aspect of Shakespearean studies. Fortunately these wonderful poems have also fos-

Bizarre theories
The numerous unlikely candidates proposed as the 'real' author of Shakespeare include Mary Queen of Scots (above), who died before any of the plays were written, and a team of Jesuits (below). In Did the Jesuits Write Shakespeare? *(1910), Harold Johnson suggested that 'Shakespeare' was a pseudonym adopted to honour Adrian IV (born Nicolas Breakspear), the only English pope.*

tered much serious and ingenious scholarship, for they pose many fascinating questions, to some of which definitive answers are unlikely ever to be found. The sonnets – 154 of them – do not form a strict sequence (and they may not have been printed in the order Shakespeare intended), but a story of sorts emerges. It involves three people: the poet; his friend, a handsome young nobleman (to whom most of the sonnets are addressed); and a dark-haired woman, the poet's mistress, who is stolen from him by his friend.

William Wordsworth, wrote of the sonnets that 'With this key Shakespeare unlocked his heart', and many other critics share his view that the poems are autobiographical. If this is so (which is by no means certain), then the identities of the young man and the 'Dark Lady' become major issues in Shakespeare's biography.

The Dark Lady?

Of all the women who have been proposed as the original of the 'Dark Lady' of Shakespeare's sonnets, Mary Fitton (left) has found the most support. Born in about 1578, she became one of Queen Elizabeth's maids of honour in 1596, and several courtiers became besotted with her. She was free with her sexual favours, but there is no evidence that Shakespeare was one of her conquests.

A possible clue to the identity of the young man is contained in the enigmatic dedication of the 1609 book: 'To the onlie begetter of these insuing sonnets Mr. W. H. . . . .' The dedication is signed (or initialled) by the printer, Thomas Thorpe, rather than by Shakespeare, and it may be that Thorpe is thanking a contact who obtained the poet's manuscript for him to print (another printer, called William Hall, has been suggested as a candidate). However, many critics assume that 'Mr. W. H.' is the young man of Shakespeare's poem, and much ingenuity has been expended in finding names to fit the initials.

Two young aristocrats have found more support than any other candidates: Henry Wriothesley, Third Earl of Southampton (whose initials must be reversed to make him 'W.H.'); and Wil-

liam Herbert, Third Earl of Pembroke. Southampton was a notable patron of literature, and Shakespeare dedicated his poems *Venus and Adonis* and *The Rape of Lucrece* to him (they are his only works to have such dedications).

Herbert was the holder of several important offices during the reign of James I, and it was to him and his brother, Philip, Earl of Montgomery, that Shakespeare's friends dedicated the First Folio edition of his works, published in 1623. Both men seem reasonably plausible candidates, then, but there is no real evidence to support their claims, and objections can easily be raised to them, not least that neither was a 'Mr', since they both had noble titles.

Shakespeare's sonnets also mention another poet, 'a worthier pen' to whom he is 'inferior far' and who is a rival for the favour of his patron. There has been much speculation about his identity. Christopher Marlowe is the favourite choice, and other contenders include George Chapman (author of a famous translation of Homer), Ben Jonson and Edmund Spenser, as well as several lesser known figures.

Even more than the Rival Poet, however, it is the Dark Lady who has caught the imagination,

Aristocratic links

William Herbert, 3rd Earl of Pembroke (above), came from a noted literary family. His mother, the sister of Sir Philip Sidney, was the finest woman poet of her age. The family home, Wilton House (above) in Wiltshire, was a meeting place for writers, and Shakespeare's company performed there in 1603, when the plague had closed the theatres in London. The circumstantial evidence that William Herbert was the 'Mr W.H.' of Shakespeare's sonnets is intriguing, but there is no firm documentary link between the two men.

and much energy has been devoted to trying to unmask this mysterious temptress who bewitches the poet and seduces his adored young friend. From the sonnets we learn that she was dark-haired, dark-eyed and dark-skinned (although how dark is uncertain – some scholars have looked for a negress to fit the bill), that she was musical and younger than the poet, and that although she was not conventionally beautiful, she was highly seductive and promiscuous.

The first person to tackle the problem was an antiquarian called George Chalmers, who, in two fat volumes published in the 1790s, attempted to show that the sonnets were addressed to Elizabeth I (even though she must have been about 60 when they were written). Like many of his successors in the Victorian age, Chalmers refused to admit the obvious fact that the sonnets have a very powerful sexual charge, and declared that Shakespeare – 'a husband, a father, a moral man' – would not have written erotic verses to a young man and a woman of easy virtue.

Of the many other women who have more plausibly been put forward as candidates for the Dark Lady, the best known is Mary Fitton, one of Queen Elizabeth's maids of honour and a notoriously promiscuous woman (in 1601 there was a scandal when she gave birth to a stillborn illegitimate child, whose father was William Herbert – possibly the Mr. W. H. of the sonnets). Mary is a strong contender in some ways, but portraits show that she had a fair complexion, and there is no evidence that she even met Shakespeare, let alone had an affair with him.

ANOTHER DARK LADY

The search therefore continues, the latest major candidate to emerge being Emilia Lanier, née Bassano, the daughter of an Italian musician. She was put forward in 1973 by the eminent but controversial Elizabethan historian A. L. Rowse, who found references to her in the manuscripts of Shakespeare's contemporary Simon Forman, a physician, astrologer, playgoer and lecher.

It appears from Forman's notes that Emilia was promiscuous, and Rowse points out that she is described in them as 'very brown in youth' and that she was married to a man called William, whose name (together with that of Shakespeare himself) figures in the many 'will' puns of the sonnets. Further investigation, however, showed that Rowse had misread Forman's notes, where Emilia is described as 'very brave' (that is 'splendid' or 'showy') not 'very brown', and that her husband was called not William, but Alfonso – a name on which even Shakespeare would have found difficulty making puns. Thus Emilia too joined the ranks of 'possibles' rather than 'probables'.

All the fervent convictions and painstaking scholarship that have gone into investigating Mr. W. H., the Rival Poet and the Dark Lady may, indeed, be nothing more than contributions to one of the greatest wild-goose chases in history, for it is quite possible that the sonnets were written as a literary exercise (such collections were highly popular), rather than as an outpouring of the soul.

There is sometimes scope for biographical speculation not only in Shakespeare's work, but also in the documents relating to him. The best-known instance is the clause in his will in which he leaves his wife (the only bequest named to her) 'my second best bed'. This has led to the conjecture that Shakespeare cared little for his wife, but according to the law of the time a widow automatically received a good share of her late husband's estate, so there was no need to specify it. The 'second best bed' was no doubt an additional, highly personal bequest – a touching remembrance rather than an indication of neglect or indifference. The best bed would normally be reserved for guests, so the bed Shakespeare left his wife was probably the one in which they slept together.

Shakespeare himself is said to have composed the inscription on his gravestone in Stratford church:

> Good friend for Jesus sake forbear
> To dig the dust enclosed here.
> Blessed be the man that spares these stones
> And cursed be he that moves my bones.

In spite of theories that the grave contains material that would shed light on the poet's life, it has never been opened. Shakespeare's personal life remains – and is ever likely to remain – a closed book.

Lady Anne Bentinck, on loan to the National Portrait Gallery, London

Shakespeare Centre Library, Stratford-upon-Avon

Enigmatic dedication
(below) The publisher of Shakespeare's sonnets, Thomas Thorpe, prefaced the book with this perplexing note, with its mysterious full stop after every word. Identifying 'Mr W.H.' has become one of the most famous pursuits in literary detection, yet it is still uncertain whether the 'onlie begetter' is the inspiration of Shakespeare's poems or the procurer of the manuscript for Thorpe.

TO.THE.ONLIE.BEGETTER.OF.
THESE.INSVING.SONNETS.
Mʳ.W.H. ALL.HAPPINESSE.
AND.THAT.ETERNITIE.
PROMISED.
BY.
OVR.EVER-LIVING.POET.
WISHETH.
THE.WELL-WISHING.
ADVENTVRER.IN.
SETTING.
FORTH.

T. T.

Shakespeare's patron
Henry Wriothesley, 3rd Earl of Southampton, was the young nobleman to whom Shakespeare dedicated his poems Venus and Adonis *and* The Rape of Lucrece, *and he is a favourite candidate for the role of the friend addressed by the poet in the sonnets. However, we do not know how close their relationship was. Shakespeare's first biographer Nicholas Rowe (1709) said that Southampton gave Shakespeare a gift of £1000 (then a huge sum), but this seems unlikely, even for so generous a lover of literature.*

SELECTED COMEDIES

Fast-moving, colourful and witty, Shakespeare's comedies poke fun at human follies and pretensions. But they remain essentially good-natured, rejoicing in the healing power of love.

A *Midsummer Night's Dream, The Taming of the Shrew* and *Twelfth Night* are three of Shakespeare's best-loved comedies, containing some of the finest roles for women he ever wrote. The plays are all concerned with love and marriage; the humour lies in the difficulties that beset the lovers in their courtship. Much of the comedy is physical, relying on tight direction and high-speed performance, as confusion and misunderstanding multiply with hilarious effect.

A MIDSUMMER NIGHT'S DREAM

The most frequently performed of Shakespeare's comedies, *A Midsummer Night's Dream* is a fantastical tale of courtship and marriage that mainly takes place in a magical "wood near Athens" one enchanted summer's night. All the fun ingredients are present: confused identity, a play within a play, mischief and pranks – and a good jibe at the conventions of courtship. The play rejoices in a wonderful, dreamlike atmosphere evoked by moonlight and fairies. Shakespeare drew on various sources for the story – including folklore and classical mythology – but the overall plot of *A Midsummer Night's Dream* is his own captivating creation.

GUIDE TO THE PLOT
The play opens at the palace of Theseus, Duke of Athens, who is about to marry. As chief administrator of the law, he is asked to help Egeus convince his daughter Hermia that she must marry Demetrius, her father's choice of suitor, rather than Lysander whom she loves. Egeus tells her that if she does not submit she has to choose between a nunnery or death. Hermia and Lysander decide to run away.

Demetrius, meanwhile, is worshipped and adored by one Helena, but he has eyes only for Hermia. In her hapless devotion, Helena tells Demetrius of the elopement and he sets off in hot pursuit, doggedly followed in turn by the unloved Helena.

Now the fairies of the wood take pause from their own raging war-of-amours to intervene. Oberon, king of the fairies, orders his lieutenant Puck to drop the juice of a magic flower into Demetrius' eyes while he sleeps, so that on waking he will fall in love with Helena. Puck mis-

> "My Oberon! what visions have I seen! / Methought I was enamour'd of an ass."
>
> TITANIA

takes Lysander for Demetrius. Oberon tries to rectify the matter by applying juice to Demetrius' eyes, with the result that both men become enamoured of Helena; Hermia is now the one spurned.

Oberon is engaged in a long-standing quarrel with Titania, his queen, because she refuses to let him have her Indian boy as his page. As a result, all Nature has been thrown into imbalance, because there is no harmony among the fairies. Oberon uses the potion to punish the sleeping Titania: she is to fall in love with the first creature she sees, the more repulsive the better.

Meanwhile, a bucolic, rowdy group of workmen have arrived in the forest. They are bent on rehearsing a performance of *Pyramus and Thisbe* as part of Duke Theseus' wedding celebrations. Falling asleep between scenes, Bottom the weaver is made the butt of Oberon's joke. Puck bestows on him the head of an ass, and when Titania wakes, she is ecstatically infatuated with the 'translated' version of Bottom.

LOVE'S FOLLY
The romanticism of the play is counterbalanced by a strong anti-romantic theme: love may be wondrous, but it can also make fools of everyone. It is constantly presented as irrational:

Noel Paton: Quarrel of Oberon and Titania (detail)/National Gallery of Scotland/Bridgeman Art Library

Strife in fairyland
At the beginning of the play Oberon, the king of the fairies, is angry with his queen, Titania, because she will not give up to him her attendant – "A lovely boy, stolen from an Indian king". With the aid of his lieutenant, Puck, Oberon plots a mischievous revenge.

Amateur theatricals
The artisans (left) who enact a play within a play are among Shakespeare's most delightful comic creations. Chief among them is Bottom, who – transformed by fairy magic – terrifies his friends (below).

Mary Evans Picture Library

Fuseli: Titania's Awakening/Kunstmuseum Winterthur/Lauros Giraudon/Bridgeman Art Library

Mary Evans Picture Library

Titania in love
(above) A magic potion makes the fairy queen fall in love with the grotesque Bottom: "thy fair large ears, my gentle joy".

Harmony restored
While the human lovers lie asleep, the fairy king and queen are reconciled (below): "Come, my queen, take hands with me."

*"Love looks not with the eyes, but with the mind;
And therefore is wing'd Cupid painted blind."*

Poor Helena, first the victim of unrequited love and then the objective of two lovers' passions, thinks she is the butt of some dreadful joke. Lysander solemnly rationalizes his change of heart, but we and the fairies know he is deluding himself. As Puck says, "Lord, what fools these mortals be!"

Titania's infatuation is explained by Bottom himself – "reason and love keep little company together now-a-days." And the irrationality of love is pressed home by Theseus at the end of the play:

*"Lovers and madmen have such seething
brains,
Such shaping fantasies, that apprehend
More than cool reason ever comprehends."*

The play then enacted by the Athenian workmen (intended to represent romantic tragedy) degenerates into farce.

Shakespeare's satire is affectionate, however. The madness of infatuation fades with the night, but, emerging from the woods, Demetrius asks, "Are you sure/That we are awake? It seems to me/That yet we sleep, we dream." Romance prevails, yet the audience has had a chance to laugh at Love's folly.

Noel Paton: Reconciliation of Oberon and Titania/National Gallery of Scotland

THE TAMING OF THE SHREW

One of Shakespeare's earlier comedies, *The Taming of the Shrew* is less sophisticated than his later work and relies on farce rather than verbal wit for its comedy. By Shakespeare's standards it is not notable for its poetry, but its tremendous gusto has made it extremely popular on stage (and more recently in film versions). The play addresses the subject of who should be the dominant partner in marriage – a common concern of literature at the time, especially of folk ballads.

GUIDE TO THE PLOT

Christopher Sly, a tinker, is roused from his drunken sleep by a lord who takes him into his house and, as a joke, treats him as

a nobleman. A play is performed for Sly's entertainment about a rich Italian called Baptista Minola and his attempt to find husbands for his two daughters. Baptista is determined that his sweet younger daughter Bianca shall not marry until fiery Katharina is wed. To win favour with Baptista, Bianca's two suitors, Gremio and Hortensio, decide to find a husband for Katharina.

Their plans are interrupted by the arrival of Lucentio and his servant Tranio. Lucentio immediately falls in love with Bianca, changes clothes with Tranio, and becomes Bianca's tutor. Meanwhile Petruchio, a friend of Hortensio, is attracted by Katharina's dowry and begins a fast and brutal courtship. He aims to break her will and make Kate submissive.

Meanwhile, Bianca is in danger of being married to Tranio, whom her father mistakes for the wealthy Lucentio.

(Tranio even persuades an old man to pose as his father and promise a large dowry.) The confusion, based on deceit and disguise, escalates rapidly until the surprising, peaceable ending.

Marriage is, of course, the dominant theme. There are four courtships and marriages to compare: Sly and his disguised page-boy 'wife'; Bianca and her three suitors; Kate and Petruchio; and, at the end, Hortensio and a certain widow. Sly is gleeful at the thought of possessing a sweet and pliant wife who addresses him as "My husband and my lord, my lord and husband". This is very much in keeping with the Elizabethan notion of marriage. Bianca may be wooed with great chivalry, her suitors being prepared to go to extreme lengths to be near her. She may inspire breathless love at first sight.

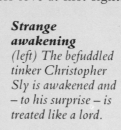

Strange awakening
(left) The befuddled tinker Christopher Sly is awakened and – to his surprise – is treated like a lord.

Suitor in disguise
(below) To gain access to Bianca, with whom he is in love, Lucentio (in the red gown) disguises himself as a tutor, for her father Baptista has decided that she should receive lessons in music and poetry.

But on marriage she is expected to be at her husband's beck and call.

Knowing the fate in store for them might explain why both Kate and Bianca asserted their independence before marriage. Bianca refuses to co-operate with her father's wishes and marries her lover in secret. Kate refuses outright to consider any man for a husband. Entirely dependent on her father, she nevertheless rebels at the notion of being 'sold' with a large dowry to the first bidder.

Method in madness
After he has married Kate, Petruchio (right) treats her like a falconer taming a wild bird, aiming to "make her come and know her keeper's call". He finds fault with everything and throws her food on to the floor. Depriving her of sleep as well as food, Petruchio gradually wears Kate down.

"Fiend of hell"
"Renown'd in Padua for her scolding tongue", Katharina (above) has frightened off prospective suitors. But Petruchio is made of stronger stuff: "Have I not in my time heard lions roar?"

Colourful conclusion
The play ends with a banquet (right) to celebrate Lucentio's marriage to Bianca. To show that he has tamed Kate, Petruchio wagers with his friends that his wife is more obedient than theirs.

Marriage is inextricably tied to money in this play. Petruchio makes no secret of his search for a generous dowry. Baptista is prepared to pay a large sum of money to someone to take Kate off his hands. Conversely, his younger daughter's suitors must pay him for the honour of marriage to Bianca.

STRENGTH AND DEFIANCE

Kate's rage and outspokenness frighten everyone off: "That wench is stark mad or wonderful froward." And a 'froward' woman is nothing "but a foul contending rebel/And graceless traitor to her loving lord." Bianca's suitors use disguise, sweet words and music in their courtship. Petruchio has other means of conquest: ". . . and so she yields to me,/For I am rough and woo not like a babe." Kate's answer to his proposal is equally aggressive: "I'll see thee hanged on Sunday first."

However strong and defiant she is, Kate is forced to capitulate to father and suitor. After their marriage, Petruchio continues his perverse and cruel 'instruction'. He treats her as he would a falcon in training: taming by starvation.

Though the suitors court differently, they all want the same after marriage – a wife who will believe that "Thy husband is thy lord, thy life, thy keeper,/Thy head, thy sovereign." Do they achieve it? Certainly Bianca has a surprise in store for her husband, and Kate's 'conversion' has been interpreted on stage as a mere pretence of wifely, loving obedience in order to outmanoeuvre her husband. But, unpalatable as actresses, students, producers and audiences may find the message today, in this play at least, Shakespeare seems to have held certain beliefs in common with Petruchio.

> *"Her only fault, and that is faults enough / Is that she is intolerable curst / And shrewd and froward . . ."*
>
> HORTENSIO

TWELFTH NIGHT

This was Shakespeare's last comedy before he embarked on his great tragedies. It is remarkable for its mixture of romanticism and boisterous comedy, combining disguise, mistaken identity, illusory passion and practical joking in a complex dramatic entertainment. The wonderfully farcical sub-plot counterbalances the main plot which at times verges on tragedy.

GUIDE TO THE PLOT

The opening scene finds Orsino, Duke of Illyria, madly in love with the Countess Olivia. She has vowed to remain secluded for seven years in mourning for her brother, but this only serves to inflame the Duke's passion. Viola arrives in Illyria, having survived a shipwreck in which she has lost her twin brother Sebastian. She disguises herself as a page called Cesario, and enters the Duke's household. Orsino is so impressed by her that he sends her to woo Olivia on his behalf.

As proxy, she proves too successful by far, and Olivia declares her love for 'Cesario', not Orsino. Viola is by now in love with Orsino, but is trapped by her disguise and must endure his wrath,

impatience and obdurate determination to be in love with the wrong woman.

The sub-plot featuring Sir Toby Belch ('kinsman to Olivia') and Sir Andrew Aguecheek, his dupe and tool, reels drunkenly in. Maria, personal maid to Olivia, devises a practical joke to play on Malvolio, the surly, conceited steward. She sends a letter to Malvolio as if from Olivia, declaring a passionate secret love for him. When Malvolio rushes to obey the instructions in the letter, his reward is to be carried off to the Elizabethan equivalent of a padded cell. Both plots merge and typical complications ensue.

A new survivor of the shipwreck makes his presence felt in Illyria. And the confusion reaches a deafening clamour before the mixed identities are unravelled and familiar romantic solutions are found.

VICTIMS OF DECEPTION

'Twelfth Night' was a traditional holiday in Elizabethan England. Such a choice of title would have conjured up ideas of festival and masquerade. The comedy lies in the bizarre and complicated misunderstandings arising out of deception and self-deception. It is a brilliantly devised comedy in which the characters carry

> "... such as I am all true lovers are, / Unstaid and skittish in all motions else, / Save in the constant image of the creature / That is beloved."   ORSINO

Mary Evans Picture Library

Merry company
Sir Toby Belch and Sir Andrew Aguecheek flank the jester Feste as they cavort merrily (above). But soon this marvellous trio – who provide much of the high-spirited fun of Twelfth Night – will be interrupted by the sour Malvolio.

Pains of love
(left) Duke Orsino is a perfect exemplar of the languishing, lovesick suitor – although he pines and frets, he also enjoys luxuriating in his passion. He sits between Viola, who is in love with him but is disguised as a boy and cannot declare her love, and Feste, who sings a sad song: "Come away, come away, death . . . I am slain by a fair cruel maid."

Walter Howell Deverell: Twelfth Night Act II Scene IV/Forbes Magazine Collection/Bridgeman Art Library

Crossed in love
(right) Malvolio has been duped by a forged letter into thinking that his mistress Olivia is in love with him. Complying with the terms of the letter, he acts and dresses ridiculously (with yellow stockings cross-gartered) and is looked on as a lunatic.

Reluctant duellers
(below) Sir Toby jokingly incites a quarrel between Sir Andrew and Cesario (Viola in disguise), knowing that each is afraid to fight.

Daniel Maclise: Malvolio and the Countess Olivia/Tate Gallery, London

Mansell Collection

away our affections by undergoing some kind of ordeal.

We are asked to swallow a great deal. Viola's remarkably successful disguise has Orsino at once confiding in her and Olivia prostrate with love, in spite of Viola's attempts to tell her "I am not what I am." But Viola, in wanting Olivia for a friend and Orsino as a lover, is somehow made plausible. On several occasions she comes close to confessing her love. She defends her assertion that women love as truly as men and tells her story as though it were that of her 'sister'. Orsino is moved and asks if her sister died of her secret love. She replies: "I am all the daughters of my father's house,/And all the brothers too: and yet I know not." Her loneliness and despair at such moments is the more appealing for being expressed obliquely.

Orsino, Olivia and Malvolio are all vic-tims of deception. The Duke is in love with the idea of loving Olivia: "O, when mine eyes did see Olivia first,/Methought she purg'd the air of pestilence." But he is speaking of a woman who will not even see him. Olivia is initially in love with the idea of mourning – and then falls for a boy who is really a girl.

DELUSIONS OF GRANDEUR
All this time, poor Malvolio is in love with himself. The scene where he imagines himself Count Malvolio – "Having been three months married to her, sitting in my state" – is hilarious. Maria's practical joke, playing on his delusions of grandeur, works brilliantly. But a modern audience feels a squirming discomfort at the humiliation which fol-lows. Malvolio's self-deception lands him in a locked, lightless cell from where he must plead his sanity to a pitiless band of practical jokers. The Elizabethan willing-ness to laugh at lunatics grates harshly and productions nowadays will go to great lengths to unseat the comedy at this point and recompense Malvolio with the audi-ence's sympathies. This in itself adds rich-ness of texture to a great comic work of art in which Shakespeare assembles light and dark, farce and poignancy, wistful song and a party mood to splendid effect.

| In the Background |

BOY PLAYERS

Much of the humour in Shakespeare's comedies lies in the confusion caused by disguise. And when a character assumes the identity of the opposite sex, as does Viola in *Twelfth Night* or Rosalind in *As You Like It* (right), the scope for comic confusion becomes the greater. In Shakes-peare's day disguise went one step further, for all actors were male; women's roles were played by boys whose voices had yet to break. The boys were apprenticed to professional players at an early age and were thoroughly trained in their craft. Shakespeare was often careful to shelter his boy players from parts they were not ready for emotionally.

Victoria and Albert Museum/Weidenfeld and Nicolson Archives

39

CHARACTERS IN FOCUS

In these comedies, where he treats the themes of love and marriage, Shakespeare creates characters ranging from the 'serious' romantic leads to buffoons. The specifically comic characters often illuminate the main relationships in each play. So the simple but shrewd Bottom remarks, for instance, "reason and love keep little company together now-a-days; the more the pity . . ."

WHO'S WHO

A MIDSUMMER NIGHT'S DREAM

Titania	The beautiful, passionate queen of the fairies.
Oberon	The all-powerful fairy "King of Shadows".
Puck	Oberon's mischievous attendant and messenger.
Bottom	A cheerful, egotistical weaver, who becomes the object of Titania's love.
Hermia, Lysander, Helena and Demetrius	Two romantic young couples, whose paths criss-cross on the tricky "course of love".

THE TAMING OF THE SHREW

Kate	The "shrew", whose sharp tongue keeps suitors at bay.
Bianca	Kate's sweet younger sister, not allowed to marry until Kate finds a husband.
Baptista	Kate and Bianca's father, a wealthy Paduan nobleman.
Petruchio	"A gentleman of Verona", determined to tame Kate.

TWELFTH NIGHT

Viola	The heroine who, in disguise, serves and loves Orsino.
Orsino	Duke of Illyria, obsessed with an unrequited passion for the Countess Olivia.
Olivia	"A virtuous maid" who is drawn to Orsino's proxy wooer, Viola.
Malvolio	Olivia's pompous steward, "an affectioned ass".
Sir Toby Belch	Olivia's uncle, fond of late-night revelling.
Sir Andrew Aguecheek	A "foolish knight", Sir Toby's drinking crony.

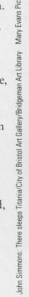

John Simmons: There sleeps Titania/City of Bristol Art Gallery/Bridgeman Art Library   Mary Evans Picture Library

Noel Paton: A Midsummer Night's Dream (detail)/Fine Art Photo Library

A MIDSUMMER NIGHT'S DREAM

The jealous fairy king, Oberon (above), and his defiant queen, Titania (below), are at odds. As a result, "The spring, the summer,/The childing autumn, angry winter, change/Their wonted liveries; and the mazed world . . . knows not which is which." Bottom the weaver (left), gets caught in the cross-fire and ends up – wearing an ass's head – in Titania's arms. An unconscious figure of fun, Bottom combines imagination and absurdity: "I have had a dream, past the wit of man to say what dream it was: man is but an ass if he go about to expound this dream . . . it shall be called Bottom's Dream, because it hath no bottom . . ."

THE TAMING OF THE SHREW

Wild and wayward, the fiery Kate (right) is determined to preserve her independence and not be made subservient through marriage. She effectively frightens off any suitors with her barbed wit: "If I be waspish, best beware my sting," she warns Petruchio. She scorns her meek sister Bianca, and Bianca's insipid swains, and regards matchmaking as little short of prostitution. But she does not hesitate to torment Bianca for her popularity and for being their father's darling.

Blown by a "happy gale" to Padua, Petruchio (far right) intends to "board" Kate as if she were a ship. Aggressive and opportunist, he is simply attracted by the size of Kate's dowry and shrugs off her fearsome reputation: "I know she is an irksome, brawling scold:/If that be all, masters, I hear no harm." Initially he pretends to find her "pleasant, gamesome, passing courteous", but rides roughshod over any protests – "will you, nill you, I will marry you." As Kate retorts, "I'll see thee hang'd on Sunday first", the scene is set for a furious struggle of wits and wills.

Columbia/Kobal Collection

F R Pickersgill: Viola and the Duke/Fine Art Photo Library

TWELFTH NIGHT

"Not yet old enough for a man, nor young enough for a boy", Viola (left), in her androgynous role, enjoys unusual freedom for a woman, but is constrained by her silent love for Orsino (left). Her forbearance contrasts with his self-indulgent obsession with Olivia. "Make no compare/ Between that love a woman can bear me/ And that I owe Olivia." But, imperceptive as he is, he recognizes signs of love in Viola. In her amatory trips between wooer (Orsino) and wooed (Olivia), the youthful but wise Viola instructs them both in the true nature of love.

Victoria and Albert Museum/Weidenfeld and Nicolson Archives

The po-faced puritan Malvolio (right) believes "that all that look on him love him". Smug, vain and ambitious, he longs to be "Count Malvolio". Deluded as to his own worth, or "sick of self-love" as Olivia puts it, he is easily duped into believing his aloof mistress is enamoured of him. Absurd and flamboyant in his pursuit of her, Malvolio in love is a hilarious caricature of the emotional turmoil experienced by the other lovers.

"THIS POWERFUL RHYME"

Shakespeare was not only the most celebrated playwright ever – he also wrote some of the finest poetry, instilled with the beauty and lyricism of his best plays.

To the Elizabethan commentator, Francis Meres, Shakespeare was 'mellifluous and honey-tongued', and to prove his point he directed people to 'witness his *Venus and Adonis*, his *Lucrece*, his sugared sonnets among his private friends'.

The works mentioned by Meres comprise most of Shakespeare's output of verse written to be read rather than performed – a fraction of his overall writing. The first two poems were reprinted frequently during and immediately after Shakespeare's lifetime, and testify to his immense popularity as a poet.

Venus and Adonis and *The Rape of Lucrece* are long, rhymed narrative poems inspired by episodes from classical myth and history, and as such mirror the Renaissance fascination with the culture of ancient Greece and Rome. In *Venus and Adonis,* the goddess of love becomes infatuated with a beautiful but ice-cold young man whom she pursues through an unmistakably English countryside. Despite the lad's untimely end, the tone is light-hearted and the verbal adroitness with which Shakespeare treated erotic ardours delighted his readers.

In the fulsome dedication of the poem to the young Earl of Southampton, Shakespeare called it 'the first heir of my invention' – ignoring the plays he had already written – and promised a 'graver labour'. This must have been *The Rape of Lucrece*, published in the following

The Rape of Lucrece
Shakespeare was fascinated by the legendary early history of Rome as told by the historian Titus Livy. In the story of Lucrece, Tarquin, the son of a tyrant and himself King of Rome, rapes the virtuous woman. Devastated, Lucrece kills herself, the Tarquins have to flee the town and Rome becomes a Republic.

Death of Adonis
(left) Shakespeare's first long narrative poem relates the tale of Venus' love for the beautiful huntsman Adonis. Her love is ill-fated, and finding him dead she howls in despair: "Alas, poor world, what treasure hast thou lost!"

Rubens: Death of Adonis/British Library/Bridgeman Art Library

year (1594) and also dedicated to Southampton. The poem reworks the semi-legendary story of the rape of the beautiful Lucrece by Tarquin, King of Rome, which resulted in Lucrece's suicide and the end of Rome's monarchy.

Its sombre subject made it less popular than *Venus and Adonis*, if we are to believe Shakespeare's contemporary, the Cambridge don Gabriel Harvey, who scribbled in the margin of a book his opinion that 'The younger sort takes much delight in Shakespeare's *Venus and Adonis*; but his *Lucrece*, and his tragedy of *Hamlet, Prince*

Titian: Tarquin and Lucretia/Fitzwilliam Museum, Cambridge

TO THE RIGHT
HONOVRABLE, HENRY
VVriothefley, Earle of Southhampton,
and Baron of Titchfield.

HE loue I dedicate to your Lordfhip is without end: wherof this Pamphlet without beginning is but a superfluous Moity. The warrant I haue of your Honourable difpofition, not the worth of my vntutord Lines makes it affured of acceptance. VVhat I haue done is yours, what I haue to doe is yours, being part in all I haue, deuoted yours. VVere my worth greater, my duety would fhew greater, meane time, as it is, it is bound to your Lordfhip; To whom I wifh long life ftill lengthned with all happineffe.

Your Lordfhips in all duety,

William Shakefpeare.

A 2

Shakespeare Centre Library, Stratford-upon-Avon

WILLIAM SHAKESPEARE

Dedication
Shakespeare dedicated The Rape of Lucrece *(left) to Henry Wriothesley, Earl of Southampton (right), to manifest the respect which he felt for his patron. But was Henry Wriothesley (HW) also the enigmatic WH to whom the passionate sonnets are dedicated?*

Hilliard/Fitzwilliam Museum, Cambridge

1592 and 1598 such sequences were extremely popular, and it is therefore usually assumed that Shakespeare's sonnets were written between these dates. Moreover Meres' reference to his 'sugared sonnets' was published in 1598, so many if not all of them must have been in circulation by that year.

As the sequence proceeds, we glimpse elements of a tale of passion and betrayal in which the poet suffers deeply. At the beginning he is passionately attached to a young man – a 'lovely boy' with 'a woman's face'. Scholars continue to argue as to whether the attachment was platonic or not, although in a number of sonnets the poet does take up the position of family friend, urging the young man to marry and beget children. Then misfortunes come thick and fast, as the friend steals the poet's mistress and adds insult to injury by taking a rival poet into his favour.

Most of the remaining sonnets are addressed to the poet's mistress, a strikingly dark married woman; the poet

Hilliard: Elizabeth of Bohemia/Private Collection/Bridgeman Art Library

dards, doubtless because Shakespeare found a fellow Stratford man, Richard Field, to do the printing.

Shakespeare's particular concern with the accuracy of the poems is attributable to the fact that in the 1590s 'pure' poetry, written for an aristocratic and intellectual élite, had far more prestige than plays composed and performed for popular entertainment. Shakespeare, who sometimes appears ashamed of being a player, may even have hoped that Southampton would find him some more 'respectable' way of earning a living. Whether or not this was so, Shakespeare remained an actor and dramatist, never again publishing anything like *Venus and Adonis*.

PRIVATE SONNETS
While the narrative poems were written for public consumption, the 'sugared sonnets' were essentially personal communications. Shakespeare intended them for circulation 'among his private friends' (as Meres noted), and their eventual publication in 1609 was almost certainly not the poet's doing. That is why the sonnets, although perhaps the greatest love poems in any language, continue to baffle all attempts to identify the situation and characters that figure in them.

A 'story' *is* involved, since the 154 sonnets are not entirely separate poems, but part of an integrated sequence. Between

of Denmark, have it in them to please the wiser sort.'

Shakespeare wrote his long poems – the only ones, so far as we know, that he ever composed – during the two years when an outbreak of plague had closed the London playhouses. His theatrical career was at a standstill, and the dedications to Southampton probably represent a determined effort on the writer's part to court and win the patronage of a great noble. One indication of his earnestness is that the published texts of the poems are unusually accurate by Elizabethan stan-

In the eye of the beholder
The 'dark lady' of Shakespeare's sonnets stood in stark contrast to conventional Elizabethan concepts of beauty (right).

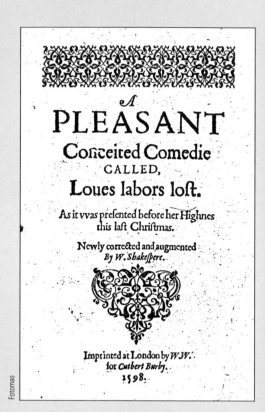

A
PLEASANT
Conceited Comedie
CALLED,
Loues labors loft.

As it vvas prefented before her Highnes
this laft Chriftmas.

Newly corrected and augmented
By *W. Shakefpere*.

Imprinted at London by *W.W.*
for *Cutbert Burby*.
1598.

Love's Labours Lost
The title page (above) marks the first occasion when Shakespeare's name appeared with the text – a departure since the Elizabethans did not view plays worthy of claims to individual authorship.

Blithe spirits
Inspired by A Midsummer Night's Dream, William Blake painted the scene (right) with Titania embracing Oberon, the King of the Fairies, while Puck suspends his magic and the fairies dance on.

praises her beauty and wit, but also draws attention to her shortcomings and abuses her bitterly for her inconstancy – "In nothing art thou black, save in thy deeds."

The identity of the chief actors in this murky drama remains one of the great literary mysteries. Many solutions have been proposed, but in every case the evidence put forward has proved to be circumstantial and incomplete.

PUNS AND WORD-PLAY
The Elizabethans admired literary virtuosity, and the sonnet owed much of its vogue to its complicated rhyme scheme – especially when puns and other forms of ingenious word-play further enlivened the text. 'Witty Shakespeare' excelled and delighted in all this; but although he was following literary fashion, there is little doubt that the actual emotions expressed in the sonnets are genuine and deeply felt. Among the most striking features are his

declarations of constancy despite betrayal ("love is not love/Which alters when it alteration finds") and his fluctuations between self-abasement and a proud assertion of his genius ("Not marble, nor the gilded monuments/Of princes shall outlive this powerful rhyme").

Although the sonnets bring us closest to the man Shakespeare, his greatest poetry is contained in the plays – not surprisingly, since as far as we know he devoted himself exclusively to drama from about 1598. Like other Elizabethan playwrights he mainly used unrhymed verse; but there are some important exceptions. Several early comedies, notably *Love's Labours Lost* and *A Midsummer Night's Dream*, contain quantities of rhyming verse whose charming springlike quality creates an appropriate atmosphere of romantic fantasy; after this, the proportion of rhymed lines in the plays declined steadily. But throughout

Music and dance
Most theatrical performances ended with a dance – usually a jig – with simple musical accompaniment (right), and A Midsummer Night's Dream and Much Ado About Nothing actually mention such dances in the text. Reputed to be a portrait of Elizabeth I joining in the revels, the painting (far right) captures the enjoyment the Elizabethans so clearly derived from dancing.

his works for the stage Shakespeare continued to scatter lovely songs; although some were popular ballads by other hands, most were probably Shakespeare's, including such famous lyrics as *Who is Silvia?*; *Sigh no more, Ladies*; *Blow, blow, thou winter wind*; and *Where the bee sucks*.

BLANK VERSE

Shakespeare's chief poetic instrument when writing speeches for his plays was blank verse, consisting of unrhymed ten-syllable lines in which the natural stress tends to fall on every second syllable: "With scóffs and scórns and cóntumélious taúnts". The overwhelming advantage of blank verse was that it charged dialogue with the emotional intensity given by the strong rhythm and pattern of verse while apparently remaining close to the flow of natural speech.

In this as in many other respects Shakespeare was fortunate in coming on the scene when he did: blank verse had been used in drama only since about 1560, and contemporaries such as Marlowe had forged it into an instrument of great dramatic power – primed and ready for a master to use to maximum effect. In Shakespeare's hands it underwent a series of changes, becoming increasingly flexible and subtle in patterning, so that long passages of his later plays might almost be described by the current 20th-century term 'free verse'.

His poetic technique was, of course, only the means through which Shakespeare channelled his extraordinary command of language and imagery and his insight into the human condition. In combining these gifts with the playwright's specific talent for creating characters and developing situations, Shakespeare produced a series of masterpieces that is unsurpassed as poetry or drama, and at this level distinctions between the two forms become irrelevant.

William Blake: Oberon Titania and Puck with Fairies dancing/Tate Gallery, London

Lyrical interludes
In Shakespeare's comedies, songs provide light, fresh interludes, ways of displaying the actor's – or choirboy's – virtuosity. In The Tempest, *Ariel (right), the magical spirit of the air, sings, sweetly "Where the bee sucks, there suck I . . ."*

J A Fitzgerald: The Release of Ariel/Fine Art Photo Library

SELECTED SONNETS

XVIII

SHALL I compare thee to a summer's day?
Thou art more lovely and more temperate:
Rough winds do shake the darling buds of May,
And summer's lease hath all too short a date:
Sometime too hot the eye of heaven shines,
And often is his gold complexion dimm'd;
And every fair from fair sometime declines,
By chance or nature's changing course untrimm'd;
But thy eternal summer shall not fade,
Nor lose possession of that fair thou owest;
Nor shall Death brag thou wander'st in his shade,
When in eternal lines to time thou grow'st:
    So long as men can breathe, or eyes can see,
    So long lives this, and this gives to life to thee.

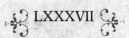

LXXXVII

FAREWELL! thou art too dear for my possessing,
And like enough thou know'st thy estimate:
The charter of thy worth gives thee releasing;
My bonds in thee are all determinate.
For how do I hold thee but by thy granting?
And for that riches where is my deserving?
The cause of this fair gift in me is wanting,
And so my patent back again is swerving.
Thyself thou gavest, thy own worth then not knowing,
Or me, to whom thou gavest it, else mistaking;
So thy great gift, upon misprision growing,
Comes home again, on better judgement making.
    Thus have I had thee, as a dream doth flatter,
    In sleep a king, but waking no such matter.

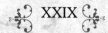

XXIX

WHEN, in disgrace with fortune and men's eyes,
I all alone beweep my outcast state,
And trouble deaf heaven with my bootless cries,
And look upon myself, and curse my fate,
Wishing me like to one more rich in hope,
Featured like him, like him with friends possess'd,
Desiring this man's art and that man's scope,
With what I most enjoy contented least;
Yet in these thoughts myself almost despising,
Haply I think on thee, and then my state,
Like to the lark at break of day arising
From sullen earth, sings hymns at heaven's gate;
    For thy sweet love remember'd such wealth brings
    That then I scorn to change my state with kings.

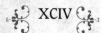

XCIV

THEY that have power to hurt and will do none,
That do not do the thing they most do show,
Who, moving others, are themselves as stone,
Unmoved, cold and to temptation slow;
They rightly do inherit heaven's graces
And husband nature's riches from expense;
They are the lords and owners of their faces,
Others but stewards of their excellence.
The summer's flower is to the summer sweet,
Though to itself it only live and die,
But if that flower with base infection meet,
The basest weed outbraves his dignity:
    For sweetest things turn sourest by their deeds;
    Lilies that fester smell far worse than weeds.

LXXIII

THAT time of year thou mayst in me behold
When yellow leaves, or none, or few, do hang
Upon those boughs which shake against the cold,
Bare ruin'd choirs, where late the sweet birds sang.
In me thou see'st the twilight of such day
As after sunset fadeth in the west;
Which by and by black night doth take away,
Death's second self, that seals up all in rest.
In me thou see'st the glowing of such fire,
That on the ashes of his youth doth lie,
As the death-bed whereon it must expire,
Consumed with that which it was nourish'd by.
    This thou perceivest, which makes thy love more strong,
    To love that well which thou must leave ere long.

CX

ALAS, 'tis true I have gone here and there,
And made myself a motley to the view,
Gored mine own thoughts, sold cheap what is most dear,
Made old offences of affections new;
Most true it is that I have look'd on truth
Askance and strangely: but, by all above,
These blenches gave my heart another youth,
And worse essays proved thee my best of love.
Now all is done, have what shall have no end:
Mine appetite I never more will grind
On newer proof, to try an older friend,
A god in love, to whom I am confined.
    Then give me welcome, next my heaven the best,
    Even to thy pure and most most loving breast.

WILLIAM SHAKESPEARE
1564-1616

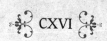 **CXVI**

LET me not to the marriage of true minds
Admit impediments. Love is not love
Which alters when it alteration finds,
Or bends with the remover to remove:
O, no! it is an ever-fixed mark,
That looks on tempests and is never shaken;
It is the star to every wandering bark,
Whose worth's unknown, although his height be taken.
Love's not Time's fool, though rosy lips and cheeks
Within his bending sickle's compass come;
Love alters not with his brief hours and weeks,
But bears it out even to the edge of doom.
    If this be error and upon me proved,
    I never writ, nor no man ever loved.

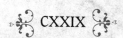 **CXXIX**

THE expense of spirit in a waste of shame
Is lust in action ; and till action, lust
Is perjur'd, murderous, bloody, full of blame,
Savage, extreme, rude, cruel, not to trust;
Enjoy'd no sooner, but despised straight;
Past reason hunted ; and no sooner had,
Past reason hated, as a swallow'd bait,
On purpose laid to make the taker mad:
Mad in pursuit, and in possession so;
Had, having, and in quest to have, extreme;
A bliss in proof, – and prov'd, a very woe;
Before, a joy propos'd ; behind, a dream:
    All this the world well knows ; yet none knows well
    To shun the heaven that leads men to this hell.

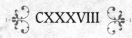 **CXXX**

MY mistress' eyes are nothing like the sun;
Coral is far more red than her lips' red:
If snow be white, why then her breasts are dun;
If hairs be wires, black wires grow on her head.
I have seen roses damask'd, red and white,
But no such roses see I in her cheeks;
And in some perfumes is there more delight
Than in the breath that from my mistress reeks.
I love to hear her speak, yet well I know
That music hath a far more pleasing sound:
I grant I never saw a goddess go,
My mistress, when she walks, treads on the ground:
    And yet, by heaven, I think my love as rare
    As any she belied with false compare.

CXXXVIII

WHEN my love swears that she is made of truth,
I do believe her, though I know she lies;
That she might think me some untutor'd youth,
Unlearned in the world's false subtleties.
Thus vainly thinking that she thinks me young,
Although she knows my days are past the best,
Simply I credit her false-speaking tongue;
On both sides thus is simple truth supprest,
But wherefore says she not she is unjust?
And wherefore say not I that I am old?
O, love's best habit is in seeming trust,
And age in love loves not to have years told:
    Therefore I lie with her, and she with me,
    And in our faults by lies we flatter'd be.

An Age of Genius

A phenomenal talent for the theatre spanned the Elizabethan and Jacobean periods and Shakespeare was simply the most brilliant dramatist of an age characterized by brilliance.

Private Collection

The Fairie Queen
Elizabeth I (left) was the Muse of the English Renaissance, credited with inspiring great chivalric love, and frequently the subject of the poetry and music produced within her Court. She herself was poet, wit and rhetorician.

War of wits
When Marlowe wrote a pastoral love poem in which a shepherd woos his love, Walter Raleigh (right) – poet and wit as well as courtier and soldier – penned a wry, practical reply from the shepherdess, pointing out the disadvantages in the shepherd's proposal.

If Shakespeare had never written a word, the period spanned by his lifetime would still be one of the great ages of English poetry and drama. During this heyday of the arts, versifying seems to have come naturally to a wide variety of people. The finest poets included not only 'literary men' such as Edmund Spenser and Michael Drayton, but also such courtly men-of-action as Sir Walter Raleigh and Sir Philip Sidney.

Whenever Queen Elizabeth travelled about the country on her 'progresses' she was greeted with declamatory verses from municipal dignitaries. She herself wrote poetry, and her thrilling speech to the troops at Tilbury on the eve of the fight against the Spanish Armada ranks among the masterpieces of English rhetoric. It includes the famous lines: 'I know I have the body of a weak and feeble woman, but I have the heart and stomach of a king, and of a king of England too.'

Shakespeare's contemporary dramatists were immensely gifted. He learned from them and they from him, for their lives and work were inter-linked. But whereas Shakespeare seems to have maintained a degree of respectability, many of his fellow dramatists led wildly bohemian lives. They kept shady company, were endlessly in debt, often in prison, and quarrelled with one another both on paper and in the flesh.

SHEER NECESSITY

This was certainly true of the 'university wits', a group of young graduates from Oxford and Cambridge with considerable talent and not much money. Robert Greene, Christopher Marlowe, George Peele, Thomas Nashe, John Lyly and others took up the hand-to-mouth existence of the professional writer and, among other achievements, began to transform the newly established Elizabethan theatre.

Robert Greene's self-destructive career is par-

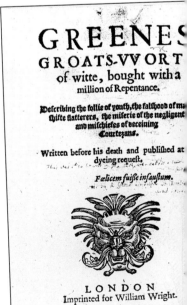

GREENES
GROATS-VVORT
of witte, bought with a
million of Repentance.

Deſcribing the follie of youth, the falſhood of makeſhifte flatterers, the miſerie of the negligent and miſchiefes of deceiuing Courtezans.

Written before his death and published at his dyeing requeſt.

Fœlicem fuiſſe infauſtum.

LONDON
Imprinted for William Wright.
1 5 9 2.

Fotomas

ers while pretending to scandalize them with detailed descriptions of the techniques used by a fraternity of thieves and con-artists: 'nips, foists, coney-catchers, cross-biters, lifts, high lawyers, and all the rabble of that unclean generation of vipers'. An unfriendly commentator pointed out that Greene had himself been enough of a crook to sell the same play to two different companies.

BARBED WIT

Greene's works for the stage were in an unexpectedly gentle, romantic vein. They were extremely popular, and by contemporary standards he was well paid for them, although he presumably spent every penny as soon as he received it. After 'a surfeit of pickled herring and Rhenish wine' he died in squalor, leaving behind a final pamphlet, *Greenes Groats-worth of Witte, bought with a million of Repentance,* supposedly written on his deathbed. In it he voices his resentment of the players, whom he sees as living securely off the labours of their betters, the university-educated writers. Even worse in Greene's eyes, was one particular player who poached on the university wits' preserves – 'an upstart crow, beautified with our feathers, that . . . supposes he is as well able to bombast out a blank verse as the best of you'. Greene makes it quite clear whom he has in mind, asserting that this player 'is in his own conceit the only Shake-scene in a country.'

Greene's death made it unnecessary for Shakespeare to answer him, although Greene's printer later made a handsome apology for his part in the publication, stating as a universally acknowledged

National Portrait Gallery, London

Greene's 'remorse'
Playwright Robert Greene (below) led a drunken, feckless life, largely financed by writing sensational pamphlets and repeatedly recanting in orgies of hack moralizing. His Groats-worth of witte (left) contains a famous attack on Shakespeare ('an upstart crow') for upstaging his better-educated contemporaries.

Bohemian life
Poets and playwrights appear to have lived on the fringes of respectability, leading wild, debauched lives in dubious company (right). The cause may partly have been that their social status was low; they were underpaid and under-valued – but their work is probably the richer for all their low-life connections and activities.

Fotomas

Mary Evans Picture Library

ticularly well known, thanks to his habit of repentantly cataloguing his sins in pamphlets written to raise cash. After taking degrees at both Oxford and Cambridge, Greene travelled around Europe, married, abandoned his wife and child once the dowry was spent, came to London, took the sister of a notorious criminal as his mistress, and lived recklessly and 'lewdly' while turning out pamphlets, romances and plays with a speed bred of necessity. Nowadays he is best remembered for the pamphlets in which he exposed the underworld which he evidently knew all too well. Like many a journalist since, he aimed to thrill his read-

fact that Shakespeare was both honourable and gentlemanly. Since Greene implied that he was a plagiarist ('beautified with our feathers'), Shakespeare may well have relished, almost 20 years later, stealing the plot of *The Winter's Tale* from one of Greene's prose romances.

Greene was about 34 years old when he died in 1592. By this time Shakespeare, at 28, was evidently beginning to make his mark as a writer of history plays, but was still overshadowed by Christopher Marlowe. A mere two months older than Shakespeare, Marlowe established himself as a major dramatist as early as 1587, when his *Tam-*

Man and superman
Christopher Marlowe (the portrait above is thought to be of him) created power-hungry heroes driven by vaulting imagination as much as ambition. Dr Faustus (left) sells his soul to the Devil for infinite knowledge and to become "great Emperor of the world". Marlowe's high-flown dramatic and poetic talent was never allowed to develop, however. He met a death almost as sudden and violent as one of his heroes', at the age of 29 at an inn in Deptford.

Theatre of blood
The huge success, between 1584 and 1589, of Thomas Kyd's revenge tragedy (right) testifies to the contemporary taste for murder, torture and violence. It contains elements which prefigure Shakespeare's Hamlet.

Shakespeare's early plays are so 'Marlovian' that some critics think Marlowe himself had a hand in them. Since Marlowe wrote for the Admiral's Men, with whom Shakespeare was also associated at the time, it is likely that they knew each other.

Unluckily for Marlowe, his genius never had time to mature. Less than a year after Greene's demise, he too was dead – killed, as it seemed, in a tavern brawl. However, various mysterious details of his life and death suggest more sinister factors at work. The clever son of a Canterbury shoemaker, Marlowe won the scholarships needed to take him through King's School, Canterbury, and Corpus Christi College, Cambridge. But his university career was punctuated by unexplained absences, and it seemed unlikely that he would be awarded his Masters' degree – until an extraordinary intervention by the Privy Council (in effect the government) changed the university authorities' decision.

'SUBTLE, SLY AND BLOODY'

The directive stated that Marlowe had been employed 'in matters touching the benefit of his country', which almost certainly means that while at Cambridge he had been recruited into the secret service. One plausible explanation for his absences is that he was abroad, posing as a Catholic in order to spy on the English seminary at Rheims. (At this time Catholic priests were viewed by the English government as Spanish agents.)

Soon after taking his Master's degree, Marlowe went to London and had an immediate success with *Tamburlaine*. He probably remained in touch with the secret service, for when he was involved

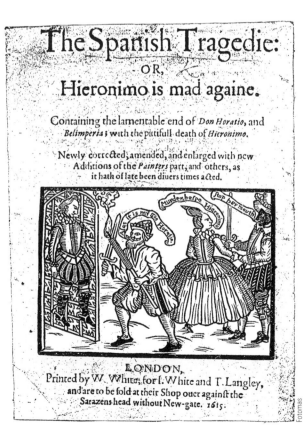

burlaine demonstrated the ornate splendour and rhetorical power that could be achieved in blank verse. 'Is it not passing brave to be a King, And ride in triumph through Persepolis?' asks the all-conquering tyrant Tamburlaine in one of many speeches that almost immediately became well-known quotations.

Marlowe's strong vein of megalomania appealed to the Elizabethan mentality. In *Tamburlaine, The Jew of Malta* and *Dr Faustus* his super-human principal characters are 'overreachers' – power-hungry anti-heroes compelled to dominate the world or master the secrets of the universe at any price. Shakespeare was to develop a much wider emotional range than Marlowe, but he undoubtedly learned a great deal from him. In fact

Ben Jonson
(above) A vital and
original force in the
Jacobean theatre, Ben
Jonson was a friend and
colleague of Shakespeare,
whom he loved 'on this
side (of) idolatry'.
Jonson's early career was
chequered by spells in
prison, first for his share
in the writing of a
'seditious' satire, and then
for killing a fellow-actor
in a duel. His great
comedies include the
darkly humorous satire
Volpone (top) in which
the main characters
personify the vice of
avarice.

in a brawl that ended with a man's death, he was not prosecuted. He evidently became a well-known figure in literary circles. He was certainly a flamboyant one, since he was openly homosexual, quarrelsome, and quick to utter flagrantly unorthodox opinions on such dangerous topics as religion. One interpretation of the events of May 1593 is that someone in authority decided that Marlowe had become a security risk and must be silenced.

The first victim, however, was another notable dramatist, Thomas Kyd. In literary history his fame rests on *The Spanish Tragedy* (produced in about 1587), a corpse-ridden piece which started a 50-year vogue for revenge plays. Kyd, a few years older than Marlowe, was not a university man, and little is known of his life except for one episode. Probably his only 'crime' was that he had shared working quarters with Marlowe. The place was raided, and among the writings discovered were some that expressed 'vile heretical conceits denying the divinity of Jesus Christ'. The unlucky Kyd was put on the rack and soon told the authorities everything they wanted to hear. The papers were Marlowe's, 'shuffled with some of mine (unknown to me)' – and, yes, Marlowe had uttered all sorts of obscene blasphemies and was, besides, a traitor.

On 18 May 1593 a warrant was issued for Marlowe's arrest, and two days later he was examined; but the only immediate result was an order that he must report daily to the authorities. On 30 May he spent a pleasant day with three companions at a Deptford tavern, got into a quarrel over the bill for supper, and was fatally injured by a stab in the eye. It is difficult to believe that this was just an accident, since all three of Marlowe's companions are known to have had links with the secret service, and Marlowe's killer was subsequently pardoned. Kyd was also released, but died a year or so later, his constitution ruined, perhaps, by torture and imprisonment.

ALCHEMICAL MAGIC

By 1594 most great English playwrights of the first generation were either dead or had turned to writing in other genres. For a few years, Shakespeare must have reigned virtually unchallenged. Then, from about the turn of the century, new men began to come forward. Thomas Dekker, John Marston, Thomas Middleton, John Webster, Francis Beaumont, John Fletcher and others were to make the Jacobean stage as lively as its Elizabethan predecessor.

Unfortunately little is known of their lives except for those occasions when they fell foul of the censorship or went to prison for debt. But one colourful figure did manage to ensure, through his opinionated writings, that both his contemporaries and posterity would take notice of him. He was Ben Jonson, and he is not least remembered for his comments on his friend William Shakespeare.

Eight years younger than Shakespeare, Jonson was the stepson of a bricklayer and was himself

Sources and Inspiration

apprenticed to the craft for a time – to his lifelong mortification, since his enemies constantly taunted him with the fact. Perhaps as a reaction, Jonson became an accomplished classical scholar, convinced that a learned 'Roman' tragedy was the highest form of dramatic art – although his own classical efforts were received with distinct indifference by Jacobean audiences. His remark that Shakespeare knew 'small Latin and less Greek' (true only by Jonson's scholarly standards) has been largely responsible for the prolonged misconception that Shakespeare was an uneducated man.

Having abandoned bricklaying, Jonson served in the Dutch war. He later boasted that in single combat he had 'slain his man in the sight of both armies'. We first hear of him on the stage in 1597, when he appeared as a (not very good) actor and spent some time in prison for his part in writing *The Isle of Dogs*. The play has not survived, so it is impossible to know how it offended the authorities. He then enjoyed his first success with *Every Man in His Humour* (1598), in which Shakespeare acted.

Over the next few years Jonson wrote prolifically and lived turbulently. He fought a duel with an actor and slew him with a 'three-shilling rapier', an action for which he narrowly escaped hanging and was branded on the thumb. Between 1599 and 1602 he took a vigorous part in 'the war of the theatres', writing several plays pillorying rival authors John Marston and Thomas Dekker, who replied in kind. (There is reference in *Hamlet*

Masques
Courtly entertainments costing vast sums of money and involving immensely complex stage machinery, masques were never seen by the common man. Their preoccupations were long-winded, classical themes combining music, poetry and visual splendour. Performances could last for several hours.
In The Masque of Blackness *(1605) by Ben Jonson, mounted at Whitehall Palace, the King's wife and ladies-in-waiting took part. Their gorgeous costumes included those shown right and below.*

Jonson and Jones
Ben Jonson began writing masques when he was creating his greatest plays for the theatre. They are a massive contradiction: Volpone, The Alchemist *and* Bartholomew Fair *are peopled with rogues, gulls, whores and beggars, while the masques were vehicles for aristocratic amateurs to play at gods and goddesses. The architect Inigo Jones designed the costumes and sets for Jonson's masques, and Jones and Jonson enjoyed a productive if volatile collaboration from* The Masque of Blackness *onwards.*

to this strangely self-indulgent interlude in English drama.) And in 1605 he found himself in prison again, along with Marston and George Chapman, for their play *Eastward Hoe!* contained jibes at the Scots that failed to amuse England's new Stuart king.

After this, Jonson managed to keep out of serious trouble. He produced his most successful plays – bitingly funny satires such as *Volpone* (1605) and *The Alchemist* (1610) – and then became involved in writing masques (pageant-like performances with splendid spectacles, costumes and music) for the court. In 1616 the forgiving King James granted him a pension, making him in effect England's first poet laureate.

In 1616, Shakespeare died at Stratford, according to one tradition, after a drinking bout with Jonson and Michael Drayton. In the same year, Jonson issued his own collected works – the very first attempt by an English playwright to assert that his writings were not ephemera but literature. Shakespeare had failed to issue such a collection, but the posthumous First Folio containing his plays would almost certainly never have been produced but for Ben Jonson's example.

Jonson's best work was done, but he still had many years to live – he died in 1637, only five years before the English theatres were closed by the Puritans. On his gravestone was carved the simple inscription, 'O rare Ben Jonson'. The age which bred him merits a similar memorial.

THE ROMANTIC POETS

WILLIAM WORDSWORTH
1770-1850

SAMUEL TAYLOR COLERIDGE
1772-1834

LORD BYRON
1788-1824

PERCY BYSSHE SHELLEY
1792-1822

JOHN KEATS
1795-1821

Reacting against the formal, rational elements of 18th-century verse, the Romantic poets changed the face of English poetry. Wordsworth and Coleridge were 'first-generation' Romantics. Byron, Shelley and Keats, who followed, were tragically short-lived – but not so their art, which encompassed some of the most lyrical and passionate of English poems.

William Wordsworth

In the course of his long life Wordsworth changed from a young rebel to a pillar of the Establishment. His literary eminence made the Lake District – where he spent most of his life – a place of pilgrimage.

Wordsworth was of the first generation of Romantic poets. His life was a model of artistic dedication and persistence – most of it spent quietly, frugally and laboriously in the Lake District, while metropolitan critics savagely abused his work. But he lived to achieve universal recognition, and in his old age became Poet Laureate.

William Wordsworth was born on 7 April 1770 at Cockermouth, a little Cumbrian market town on the edge of the Lake District. He lost his mother when he was seven, but his schooldays at Hawkshead were happy. However, when his father died in 1783, the five young Wordsworths found themselves impoverished and dependent on the charity of relatives. William was sent to St John's College, Cambridge, but, rapidly disillusioned by university life, deliberately neglected his studies. Despite his slender resources, he refused to take up a conventional career, dedicating himself to poetry and adopting radical opinions.

On a visit to France and Switzerland in 1790, he was fired by popular enthusiasm for the French Revolution. Returning to France in 1791, Wordsworth had a love affair, at Orléans, with a girl named Annette Vallon, who bore him a daughter. Later in 1792 he left for England to raise money, possibly intending to go back and marry Annette; but war broke out between Britain and France, ending the relationship by cutting off all communications for years. This episode in the poet's life remained a closely guarded secret until the 1920s.

A CHANGE OF FORTUNES

Wordsworth's early publications had aroused little interest, but a turning point in his fortunes occurred in 1795, when a young admirer died and left him £900 – enough for the 'plain living and high thinking' that appealed so strongly to Wordsworth. It was also enough to support his sister Dorothy, who could now share his home and become his closest companion. Dorothy Wordsworth proved to be a remarkable observer, and her journals – works of literature in their own right – often serve as source-books for the background of such famous poems as William's *Daffodils*.

At about this time, the poet Samuel Taylor Coleridge also entered Wordsworth's life. William and Dorothy became the Coleridges' neighbours at Nether Stowey in Somerset, and the two poets stimulated each other to an intense pitch of creativity. Local antagonism to their bohemian lifestyle and radical friends eventually persuaded them to move on.

To finance a trip to Germany, Wordsworth and Coleridge published *Lyrical Ballads* (1798), a selection of their work now recognized as a landmark in English poetry. Nineteen out of the 23 poems were by Wordsworth, although the volume appeared anony-

The aged poet
(right) Ironically, as Wordsworth's imaginative powers declined, his popularity soared. Passionate youth gave way to sober middle age in his poetry and personality alike, but the public lionized him. However, his younger contemporaries Byron and Shelley mocked the simplicity of his poetry, and deplored him as a reactionary.

A devoted sister
(left) One year younger than William, Dorothy Wordsworth lived with her brother from 1795 until his death 55 years later. Coleridge described himself, Dorothy and William as 'three people with one soul'.

mously. ('Wordsworth's name is nothing', Coleridge explained, 'and mine stinks.') Wordsworth's intention was 'to choose incidents and situations from common life, and to relate or describe them, throughout, as far as possible in a selection of language really used by men'. But although the collection contained masterpieces such as *Tintern Abbey*, it received just three reviews and sold only a handful of copies.

The German trip was also a failure, and William and Dorothy returned to England in February 1799. They settled in the Lake District, and rented – for £8 a year – the most famous of all their homes, Dove Cottage in Grasmere. The years at Dove Cottage (1800–08) saw

Love and loyalty

(above) Wordsworth first
met his wife Mary when
they were at infants' school
together. They were married
for almost 50 years, and had
five children – two of whom
died tragically in the same
year, 1812.

Walking tour

In 1799 Wordsworth and
Coleridge walked from
County Durham to the
Lake District – crossing
Greta Bridge (below).
Wordsworth shared
with his friend the scenes
described in The Prelude.

Rydal Mount

(below) Wordworth's move
to his grand home, Rydal
Mount, coincided with his
assumption of the
government post of
Distributor of Stamps for
Westmorland. He lived in
this 'modest mansion of sober
hue' until his death in 1850.

Wordsworth at his creative peak. Many great poems
from this period, such as *Intimations of Immortality*,
chronicle moments of almost mystical rapture that
were to become increasingly rare with the years.

Time made Wordsworth a more staid, less inspiring
figure. In 1802 he married Mary Hutchinson, a woman
he had known since childhood, and fathered five children. He became a political reactionary, now attacked
as a turncoat by younger radicals such as Byron and
Shelley. In 1813 he accepted a post – from the Govern-

ment he had once detested – as Distributor of Stamps
for Westmorland, and moved into his last and grandest
home, Rydal Mount. The government post brought
him the healthy sum of £400 a year, and in his later life
he was a wealthy man; in 1827 his friend Sir George
Beaumont, a noted patron of the arts, left him a legacy,
and in 1842 he was awarded a pension of £300 a year.

FAME AND HONOURS

By this time Wordsworth had become one of the most
famous and honoured of English writers, for the critics
had started eating their words and hailing him as a great
poet in about 1820. Thomas de Quincey, author of
Recollections of the Lake Poets (1834–39), summed up his
friend's change of fortunes when he wrote: 'Up to 1820
the name of Wordsworth was trampled underfoot;
from 1820 to 1830 it was militant; from 1830 to 1835 it
has been triumphant.' An increasingly venerated
figure, Wordsworth composed a *Guide to the Lakes*
(1822) and in old age became one of the district's chief
tourist attractions. He outlived all his great contemporaries to become Poet Laureate in 1843, seven years
before his death on 23 April 1850.

A few months later, Mary Wordsworth published
the most ambitious of all her husband's works – *The
Prelude* – completed years before but reserved for posterity. This record of 'the Growth of a Poet's Mind'
made a fitting climax to the whole of the English
Romantic movement.

Samuel Taylor Coleridge

Eloquent, idealistic and with wide-ranging talents, Coleridge nevertheless failed to find the love and fulfilment he craved – except, perhaps, in his inspiring friendship with the Wordsworths.

Coleridge's brilliant mind and eloquent tongue fascinated almost everyone who met him. Wordsworth, though often impatient with his friend's weaknesses, described him as 'the most wonderful man I have ever known'. Although Coleridge's splendid genius began to flag early in life, undermined by opium and unhappiness, he left a handful of magical, incantatory poems that place him among the greatest spirits of English literature.

Samuel Taylor Coleridge was born on 21 October 1772 at Ottery St Mary in Devon. On the death of his father, the village vicar and schoolmaster, he was sent to Christ's Hospital, a London school where he rapidly attracted attention as a prodigious scholar, omnivorous reader and spellbinding conversationalist. At Jesus College, Cambridge, he seemed certain of a great future, until events revealed the flaws in his curiously helpless, childlike character. In debt and rejected by Mary Evans, the girl he loved, Coleridge ran away and joined a regiment of dragoons under the fanciful name Silas Tom-kyn Comerbacke. Although discovered and bought out by his elder brother, he failed to settle down again at Cambridge and left without taking a degree.

Another curious episode occurred shortly afterwards, at Bristol, when Coleridge fell in with another poet, Robert Southey. These two idealistic young men planned to set up a utopian community in the wilds of America. Since there would have to be women in the community, they rather hastily became engaged to two sisters, Sara and Edith Fricker. Coleridge evidently had qualms about the arrangement, drifted off to London and even proposed again – without success – to Mary Evans. But when Southey tracked him down, Coleridge tamely allowed himself to be taken back and wedded to Sara Fricker. The utopian community never materialized, and Coleridge soon discovered that he and his wife were hopelessly mismatched.

The couple settled close to the Quantock Hills, at Nether Stowey in Somerset. By now, Coleridge had produced a political journal, *The Watchman*, and toyed

Spiritual pilgrimage
Coleridge (left) was the son of the vicar of Ottery St Mary in Devon (below) and seemed destined to follow in his father's clerical footsteps. But with his new friend Robert Southey, the 21-year-old Coleridge was captivated by the idea of a utopian community, one of whose main precepts was complete religious freedom. Later in life, however, Coleridge reappraised his unorthodox views and spent his last years studying the Bible and writing extensive commentaries on it.

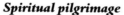

Wordsworth's sister-in-law. But Coleridge's unfulfilled relationship with her gave him little happiness, and it was to her that he addressed *Dejection: An Ode*, which has been called the saddest poem in the language. It was also to be his last major poem.

Racked by illness and hopelessly addicted to opium, Coleridge seemed to be deteriorating fast. In 1804 he went to Malta for three years as secretary to the governor, but returned in no better health and spirits. He separated from his wife, and for two years lived with the Wordsworths at Dove Cottage – a relatively stable episode during which he regularly brought out a periodical, *The Friend*, dictated to Sara Hutchinson.

When Sara left the Lake District, Coleridge moved to London. He was to be deeply wounded by Wordsworth's reported remarks about his trying domestic habits, and the ensuing breach between the two poets was never fully healed. Despite his apparent decline, Coleridge was to live for many years, mainly thanks to Dr James Gillman, who in 1816 took him into his own family and looked after him until the poet's death on 25 July 1834.

In his later years, Coleridge had made a new reputation as a lecturer and produced much distinguished philosophical and critical writing, including a famous literary autobiography, *Biographia Literaria* (1817). His poetic output was tiny compared with his fellow-Romantic Wordsworth, yet it includes at least two of the most famous and most frequently anthologized poems in the English language.

Fruitful friendship
In 1797 the Wordsworths rented Alfoxden Park (left) near Nether Stowey in Somerset in order to he near Coleridge. The two poets talked, walked and wrote, roaming the Quantock Hills for inspiration.

Wife and daughter
Against his better judgement, Coleridge married Sara Fricker (below left) in 1795. He separated from her some years later, having fathered three sons and Sara (below), who grew into a great beauty and intellectual.

with the idea of becoming a Unitarian minister. His association with William and Dorothy Wordsworth, however, reaffirmed and revitalized his poetic vocation. Coleridge contributed only four poems to *Lyrical Ballads*, of which 'it was agreed, that my endeavours should be directed to persons and characters supernatural, or at least romantic'. But one of these poems was an awesome parable-like story of unsurpassed potency, *The Rime of the Ancient Mariner*.

In 1797, Coleridge stayed for a time at a farm near Porlock in Somerset. There, according to a note he wrote in 1816, suffering from 'a slight indisposition' for which he had taken laudanum (opium in liquid form), he fell into a reverie or drugged dream in which he 'read' a long poem about the Khan Kubla. On waking, he began to write it down but, according to his own account, he was interrupted by 'a person from Porlock' and lost the thread. Wildly beautiful, exotic and enigmatic, *Kubla Khan* remained a fragment – but, nevertheless, an imperishable masterpiece.

In 1800 Coleridge and his family moved to Keswick in order to be closer to the Wordsworths. Another strong attraction of Grasmere was Sara Hutchinson,

Lord Byron

Byron was both famous and infamous for his audacious poetry, his scandalous love life and his devotion to liberal ideals. Ostracized by English society, he died fighting for Greek independence.

The family seat
(above) Newstead Abbey in Nottinghamshire came into Byron's possession when, at the age of ten, he inherited the title and estate of his great-uncle, the 5th Lord Byron. The building, which had originally been presented to the Byrons by Henry VIII in the 16th century, was in a semi-ruined state, but the young Byron fell in love with its romantic atmosphere. In 1818, however, he sold Newstead for almost £100,000 to pay off his debts.

B yron made a unique impression on 19th-century Europe, not only as a poet but as a legendary personality: a great lover and solitary brooding outsider, set against a landscape of wild romantic scenery. The real Byron was more complex, alternating his romantic role with that of a fashionable society man, and writing sustained masterpieces of comic and satirical verse.

George Gordon Byron was born on 22 January 1788 in a furnished room in London. His mother, a Scottish heiress, had seen most of her money spent by her wild, fortune-hunting husband, Captain John Byron. The young family fled from its creditors to Aberdeen, and the Captain soon decamped to France, where he died.

Until he was ten, Byron was sent to school in Aberdeen, and meanwhile a succession of doctors tried in vain to correct his deformed right foot, of which he was always to be morbidly conscious. Byron's lameness may account for his need to prove himself in love and action, and it became an important element of his romantic image.

An unexpected death promoted Byron to the ranks of the aristocracy as Baron Byron of Rochdale, with Newstead Abbey as his family seat. He was sent to Harrow, and went on to Trinity College, Cambridge, graduating in 1808. He appeared to be a typical Regency buck, deep in debt and prone to reckless dissipation, but he was also publishing a good deal of verse. When the *Edinburgh Review* dismissed it with scorn, he lashed out at the criticism in a long, immensely funny poem

entitled *English Bards and Scotch Reviewers* (1809).

In July 1809, Byron left England on a Mediterranean tour which lasted for two years. He was delighted with the exotic, untamed Balkans, and above all with Greece. 'If I am a poet,' he said, 'the air of Greece has made me one.' Back in England, he spoke out in the House of Lords against government repression of working-class discontent. Then in March 1812 he published the first two cantos of *Childe Harold's Pilgrimage*, which narrates the travels and adventures of the first distinctive 'Byronic' hero – whom contemporaries rightly assumed to be a disguised self-portrait. *Childe Harold* made Byron famous virtually overnight, and gave added allure to his extraordinary good looks and mercurial character. One of the many women who pursued him was the unstable Lady Caroline Lamb. Despite her famous description of him as 'mad, bad,

Indiscreet passions
(right and below) Byron insisted that he was the victim, rather than the seducer, of women, but his stormy love life shocked his contemporaries. His most famous affair was with Lady Caroline Lamb (below), and he is rumoured to have had an incestuous relationship with his adored step-sister Augusta (right), and to have had a child with her.

David Allan: Roy Miles Fine Paintings/Bridgeman Art Library

meanwhile, had given birth to Byron's daughter, Allegra. Mother and child travelled to Italy with the Shelleys in 1818, and Byron took on responsibility for Allegra's care. He put the little girl in a convent. But she died of typhus at the age of five.

In 1819 Byron met Teresa, the 19-year-old wife of the elderly Count Guiccioli. They became lovers, and Teresa eventually left her husband. For several years Byron led a relatively settled life with Teresa. But in 1823 he answered appeals to help the Greek revolt against Turkish rule. He was financing and training troops at Missolonghi when he fell ill with a fever. After ten days' illness, on 19 April 1824, a clap of thunder rang out and the Greeks in the streets of the town looked at one another and said, "The great man is gone." Byron had died, but in that moment a legend was born.

An exotic image
(left) Byron had a fascination with the colour and romance of the East and of the more remote areas of Europe, and he delighted in having himself painted in exotic costume. He was proud of his remarkable good looks, but he was also highly self-conscious about his club-foot, which is here artfully concealed by the draperies among which he reclines.

Greece's sufferings
(below) Byron was not the only celebrity who felt compassion for the Greeks in their fight for freedom against the Turks; artists and intellectuals all over Europe sympathized with their plight. The great French Romantic painter Eugène Delacroix painted this picture of the victims of a Turkish massacre in 1824, the year in which Byron died in Greece.

and dangerous to know', she created a series of public scandals in her frantic attempts to hold on to him.

Over the next few years, *The Giaour*, *The Corsair* and similar narrative poems, with eastern settings and mysterious, tormented heroes, reinforced the Byronic image. Yet Byron himself was trying to settle down, and in January 1815 he married Annabella Milbanke. She bore him a daughter but the marriage broke down within 15 months. Annabella, a rather solemn intellectual woman, had no idea how to handle Byron's moods and erratic behaviour.

Stung by the campaign of innuendo and insult that followed his separation from Annabella, Byron left England – as it proved, for ever – on 24 April 1816. He had already succumbed to the determined attentions of Claire Clairmont, who renewed their relationship in Switzerland and introduced Byron to her step-sister Mary, and Percy Bysshe Shelley. The poets struck up a friendship, living as neighbours at Lake Geneva.

After Shelley returned to England, Byron settled in Italy. The sale of Newstead Abbey cleared his debts, and his prolific literary output brought in huge sums. Everyone was reading Byron, though his reputation was such that a lady novelist fainted with fright in a salon when his name was announced. In the summer of 1818 he began *Don Juan*, a long, rollicking novel-like poem in which he perfected a discursive conversational style that enabled him to treat every subject under the sun. This, rather than his gloomy romantic narratives, is now regarded as Byron's master-work. Claire,

Louvre/Réunion des musées nationaux

Percy Bysshe Shelley

An atheist and radical, Shelley spent his life in virtual exile for his beliefs. Before his early death, he had stamped his unique intelligence and optimistic political vision on a series of pamphlets, essays and poems.

Shelley was above all an idealist, and in his restless, complicated private life, ideals and realities constantly clashed. His poetry is a reflection of this conflict – exalting personal and political freedom but also mirroring Shelley's own struggles with failure and disillusion.

Percy Bysshe Shelley was born on 4 August 1792 at Field Place in Sussex. His family were wealthy members of the gentry, and Shelley was sent to Eton and Oxford where he became a fine classical scholar. But he was a rebel and misfit even at school, where he was bullied mercilessly. As one schoolmate reported, 'I have seen him surrounded, hooted, baited like a maddened bull, and at this distance of time I seem to hear ringing in my ears the cry which Shelley was wont to utter in his paroxysm of revengeful anger.'

At Oxford, Shelley published a pamphlet entitled *The Necessity of Atheism*, for which he was sent down. At 18, the future poet was already a political radical, a vegetarian, an apostle of free love, and an atheist. He was also a tousled eccentric, subject to hallucinations and fits of sleep-walking, but his transparent sincerity and enthusiasm won over most of the people he met.

In London, Shelley encountered Harriet Westbrook, who attended the same boarding school as his sisters. They eloped and were married in Edinburgh on 28 August 1811. Shelley was 19, and Harriet 16. From this time, Shelley led a wandering life, rarely staying in the same place for more than a few months. Having quarrelled with his father, he was often short of money and deep in debt.

During a stay in Dublin, Shelley wrote pamphlets denouncing English rule in Ireland and discrimination against Catholics. He and Harriet lived variously in Wales, England and Scotland, while Shelley composed *Queen Mab*, his first sustained poetic statement.

Meanwhile, the incompatibility between Shelley and Harriet had become increasingly obvious – to Shelley, at least. Though Harriet was pregnant with their second child, he left her for Mary Godwin, the daughter of two people Shelley admired intensely: the radical philosopher William Godwin and his long-dead wife, the feminist Mary Wollstonecraft. In July 1814, Shelley and Mary eloped to the Continent, accompanied by Claire Clairmont, daughter of Godwin's second wife. Shelley had already displayed a taste for group living, and Claire was to stay with him and Mary for years.

Lack of money brought Shelley and his companions back to England within six weeks, but in 1816 they set out again for Switzerland. Claire Clairmont steered them to Lake Geneva, where she hoped to resume her affair with Lord Byron (she was already pregnant by

Florentine vistas
Enamoured of Italy, Shelley composed 'Ode to the West Wind' near the banks of the river Arno (above). And when his only surviving son was born there in November 1819, he and Mary named him Percy Florence to commemorate the place of his birth – which Shelley designated 'the most beautiful city I ever saw.'

Romantic impression
(left) This image of Shelley captures the essence of Romanticism – at one with Nature, a solitary figure, windswept, gaunt, deep in thought, with gnarled trees in the background. On the title page are the mythical figures of Shelley's imagination.

Eton schooldays
Shelley's time at Eton (above) was not happy – his fellow students ostracized him for his studiousness, and his tutors were outraged by his interest in black magic, finding him on several occasions surrounded by fire, apparently intent on 'raising the Devil'.

Signorini: Gavin Graham Gallery/Bridgeman Art Library

Jane Williams
(below) Shelley was one of Jane Williams' many admirers, writing poems to her such as 'When the lamp is shattered'. Later, when both he and her husband had lost their lives, Mary Shelley seems also to have fallen under Jane's extraordinary spell.

Portrait by George Clint: Bodleian Library, Oxford

him). The two poets met and formed an important, stimulating friendship. A tour of the lake with Byron inspired Shelley to compose his first unmistakably great poem, *Hymn to Intellectual Beauty*.

In September 1816 Shelley returned to England. Three months later the unlucky Harriet, pregnant by an army officer, drowned herself. Shelley and Mary were married a few days later, but this gesture towards respectability failed to procure Shelley the custody of his children by Harriet.

After a year in England, Shelley was in poor health, stifled and discouraged by the atmosphere of political repression. In March 1818 the Shelleys, their children and Claire Clairmont left for Italy, where renewed contact with Byron inspired Shelley's *Julian and Maddalo*, a vivid verse portrait of the two men. Shelley was now at the height of his powers, and *Prometheus Unbound*, *The Cenci*, *Ode to the West Wind* and *The Mask of Anarchy* were all composed in 1818–19. Much of his late verse was political, but in May 1821 the news of Keats' death prompted the elegaic *Adonais*.

THE FINAL JOURNEY
By this time, Shelley's relations with Mary were often strained. All but one of their children died, and Shelley continued to find inspiration in other women, the last one being Jane Williams to whom he wrote many poems, including 'When the lamp is shattered'.

Edward and Jane Williams were new friends who moved in with the Shelleys in April 1822 and shared their home at Lerici, on the Bay of Spezia. Although unable to swim, Shelley had a life-long passion for the water, and he intended spending the summer sailing with Edward Williams and Byron. But on 8 July, on a trip from Livorno to Lerici, Shelley's boat disappeared. Ten days later, the bodies of Shelley, Williams and their boat boy were washed ashore. Shelley was identified by the copy of Keats' poems in his pocket. Byron was one of the small party that was present when the remains of his friend were cremated on the beach. At his death, Shelley was not quite 30.

The fateful voyage
Edward Williams shared with Shelley a love of the sea, and the two eagerly awaited delivery of their boat – Williams even painted her (below), in full, resplendent sail. Their first trip, however, was to be their last. Sailing from Leghorn on 8 July 1822, they were caught in a storm and drowned.

Edward Williams: British Museum/Shelley Museum, Bournemouth

John Keats

Although his life was tragically short, Keats was blessed with a "teeming" poetic gift which triumphed over both his personal suffering and savage criticism.

Keats was the youngest of the great Romantics, and the first to die. Yet because of his precociously mature genius, he left a substantial body of work, including poems whose sensuous loveliness demonstrates his cherished belief that Beauty and Truth are one and the same.

John Keats was born in London on 31 October 1795. His father ran a prosperous livery stable in the parish of Moorfields, and at the age of seven Keats was sent to a good private school at Enfield. But both his parents died by the time he was 14, and in 1810 his guardian apprenticed him to a surgeon and apothecary at Edmonton, Middlesex. Although he qualified in 1816 and spent a few months studying surgery at Guy's Hospital, the lure of poetry proved too strong for Keats. For the rest of his brief life he lived precariously as a professional writer, sometimes desperately short of money and working with great intensity while his health lasted.

A PRECOCIOUS GENIUS

As a teenager Keats steeped himself in English poetry, and his first efforts at verse – probably made at about 18 – were predictably lush and imitative. But by 1816 he was maturing fast. In April, Leigh Hunt's magazine *The Examiner* published Keats' sonnet *To Solitude*. By the end of the year he had shown further skill and subtlety with *On First Looking into Chapman's Homer* (a poem about a poem – George Chapman's

Joseph Severn
A true friend to Keats, Joseph Severn (right) was a frequent visitor at his house, and the only one of their circle who was prepared to leave England for Italy when Keats' health failed. In Rome, Severn tended him night and day, cooking, reading to him, and trying to make his final days as comfortable as possible. He even reputedly stopped Keats from committing suicide on one particularly bleak occasion. Severn painted Keats in this sensitive pose (far right) during their last days together.

Self-portrait. National Portrait Gallery

Joseph Severn, National Portrait Gallery

early 17th-century translation of the *Iliad* and the *Odyssey*), and Hunt was confidently prophesying greatness for him.

Leigh Hunt, himself a distinguished essayist and journalist, gave Keats invaluable encouragement, introducing the inexperienced young poet to his literary circle, which included Shelley and the critic William Hazlitt. However, most of these men were regarded as dangerous radicals by powerful establishment periodicals such as *Blackwood's*, and Keats was later to suffer for his association with what they sneeringly labelled 'the Cockney school of poetry'.

When his first collection of poems appeared in

March 1817, it was ignored rather than abused. Not discouraged, Keats moved out of London to Hampstead – then a country village – and worked for months on an epic poem, *Endymion*. The result was flawed in parts, but the disciplined effort involved seems to have brought Keats to the verge of his astonishingly early artistic maturity. In the spring of 1818, he completed another long narrative poem, *Isabella; or, the Pot of Basil*.

That summer, Keats and a friend embarked on a 42-day walking tour of the Lake District, Ulster and Scotland which overtaxed the poet's strength. When he reached Inverness, a local physician insisted that he

John Varley, Keats House, Hampstead

Hampstead Heath
During the winter of 1816-17, Keats left London and joined his brothers in the village of Hampstead (left), to be near his friend and fellow-writer Leigh Hunt. The Heath was his back garden, and he delighted in strolling across it, watching the wind ruffling great fields of barley like the motion of "the inland sea".

Roman requiem
With books and a piano to distract him, Keats spent his final weeks in a corner room beside the Spanish Steps in Rome's Piazza di Spagna.

return home at once. This ominous incident was followed by the death of Keats' brother Tom, whom he nursed devotedly through the last stages of consumption – the disease that was, in the space of three short years, to take the poet's own life.

Meanwhile, the Tory reviewers had begun to single out Keats for attack. *Blackwood's* snobbishly derided the poetic efforts of footmen, farm-servants and apothecaries, sardonically lamenting 'the calm, settled, imperturbable drivelling idiocy of *Endymion*'. It advised, 'It is a better and wiser thing to be a starved apothecary than a starved poet; so back to the shop Mr John, back to the "plasters, pills and ointment boxes".'

Shelley's *Adonais* implies, and legend has it, that such savagery broke Keats' heart and killed him. In reality, the reviews appeared just when he was entering his 'Great Year', 1818-19, when he produced one masterpiece after another, including *Hyperion*, *The Eve of St Agnes*, all his great Odes, such as *Ode to a Nightingale*, and *La Belle Dame Sans Merci*.

After this supreme creative output, Keats was unwell

Keats House, Hampstead

Keats' love
Fanny Brawne (left), who met Keats in November 1818, was five years younger than the poet. Keats was immediately and completely enthralled by her, expressing his passion in many poems and letters. She was the "sweet home of all my fears,/ And hopes, and joys, and panting miseries . . ." They became secretly engaged in 1819, but his illness marred what happiness they might have had. She wore mourning for several years after his death, but finally married in 1833.

in the winter of 1819-20, and in February 1820 began to cough blood. He immediately recognized this as his 'death warrant'. The blow was all the more cruel because he had met and become engaged to a young neighbour named Fanny Brawne. Their relationship was stormy, since Keats, realizing he was to die, suffered agonies of jealousy. But it was among the Brawne family that he spent his last weeks in England.

A PAINFUL DEATH
By September 1820 Keats' condition was desperately serious, and his friends believed that only the Southern sun might cure him. A close friend, the painter Joseph Severn, travelled with him to Rome, and the two men took rooms on the Piazza di Spagna, at the bottom of the Spanish Steps. Here, after terrible suffering, Keats died in Severn's arms on 23 February 1821. He was buried in Rome's Protestant cemetery, where his tombstone was inscribed, as he had instructed, with the gloomy words 'Here lies one whose name was writ on water.' But his name has not disappeared – posterity has endorsed his defiant response to the reviewers: 'I think I shall be among the English poets after my death.'

SELECTED POEMS

One work from each of the Romantic poets illustrates the wide range of their individual styles and concerns. Other major poems are discussed in the captions.

The Romantic poets' freshness of language, personal intensity and splendour of vision transformed the English poetic tradition. Yet although they are now viewed as forming a 'school', their differences are as striking as their similarities.

Wordsworth's *Intimations of Immortality* focuses on the inspiration he found in Nature, but Coleridge's *The Ancient Mariner* evokes the surreal world of the unconscious mind. Both these poets are among the targets of Byron's scathing humour in *Don Juan*. And while Shelley's *The Mask of Anarchy* is a protest about a recent massacre, Keats' *Ode to a Nightingale* deals with timeless questions about life, death, and the nature of experience.

✥ *Wordsworth* ✥

Ode: Intimations of Immortality

Wordsworth's major source of poetic inspiration – his visionary response to Nature – deserted him when he was in his early 40s. He foresaw the loss much earlier, and his Ode entitled *Intimations of Immortality from Recollections of Early Childhood,* begun when he was 32, revolves around this creative and spiritual crisis.

The Ode can be divided into three sections. In stanzas I-IV Wordsworth writes of his joyful sense of communion with the natural world, and asks where "the visionary gleam" has gone. In stanzas V-VIII he elaborates on the theory of immortality or 'pre-existence', whereby children enter this world with a memory of another, eternal, life-before-birth. This sense of an invisible world was what the young Wordsworth achieved in his poetic imagination; the sense fades as children grow up, just as Wordsworth's own mystical relationship with Nature was fading. In stanzas IX-XI, the poet consoles himself with the realization that he can still respond deeply to Nature.

"Tintern Abbey" reveals the poet's changing response to Nature. His "dizzy raptures" are replaced by a sense of Nature as a moral guide.

GLOSSARY

Allegory: a story where the characters and incidents have a meaning beyond the literal
Augustan: a term applied to the early 18th century in England, a period of refinement and classicism. It refers back to the brilliant literary age of the Roman Emperor Augustus
Ballad: a poem that tells a story, originally set to music. Simple and rhythmic in form
Canto: a major subdivision of an epic, like a chapter in a book
Couplet: two successive lines of verse, particularly when they are rhymed
Epic: long poem narrating the adventures and achievements of a heroic figure
Lyric: in ancient Greece, a song put to the music of the lyre. Any poem set to music, or a short poem expressing strong emotion or sensation
Ode: a poem written to celebrate a person or thing. Originally intended to be sung
Picaresque: relating to a rogue's adventures
Satire: the exposure of vice or folly by ridicule
Stanza: group of two or more lines in a poem – effectively a verse

Childlike joy
(left) Wordsworth's special poetic gift was that he could see the world with the freshness and wonder of a child. For him, children's unfettered delight in Nature held the key to creativity. He knew that his unique gift would not last, and Intimations of Immortality *centres on that disturbing premonition.*

"My heart leaps up when I behold A rainbow in the sky"
Wordsworth wrote this little poem the day before he began the Ode; he used its last three lines as a preface. It may be the "timely utterance" to which he refers in the Ode's third stanza. He seems sure of his inspiration in these lines, but the next day he was suffering a crisis of confidence.

James Barras: Paddling. Fine Art Photographic Library

Turner: Kilchern Castle, Plymouth Art Gallery

Wordsworth prefaced his Ode with three lines from a little poem which he wrote on the previous day, 26 March 1802. This poem, which begins "My heart leaps up when I behold/A rainbow in the sky", revealed that he had not entirely lost his childlike rapture in the presence of the mysteries of Nature. But he knows that this gift is beginning to fade. The anguish of that knowledge is expressed in the immensely sad, echoing final lines of the first two stanzas: "The things which I have seen I now can see no more", and "That there hath passed away a glory from the earth." Nature itself has not changed – the Rainbow, the Rose, the Moon, the sunshine are still "glorious"; what has changed is Words-worth's own ability to see "every common sight . . . apparelled in celestial light."

In stanza III, Wordsworth describes how his delight in Nature is interrupted by a ter-rifying "thought of grief" – the thought that he might lose his poetic inspiration. But a "timely utterance" (an inspired poem?) "gave that thought relief", and his determined, almost desperate, joy gains momentum throughout the rest of the stanza and into the 4th, mounting up through "I have heard the call", "I feel – I feel it all" to the climactic "I hear, I hear, with joy I hear!" But despair sud-denly rips through the rhetoric, demanding

Whither is fled the visionary gleam?
Where is it now, the glory and the dream?

Then Wordsworth sets out the strange, but beautiful notion of a life–before–birth:

Not in entire forgetfulness,
And not in utter nakedness
But trailing clouds of glory do we come
From God, who is our home:
Heaven lies about us in our infancy!

Gradually the divine vision fades "into the light of common day"; just as inspired imagi-nation declines into poetic dullness. But still Wordsworth can find reassurance in "the little Child" – "thou Eye among the blind".

In the poem's final stanzas, the poet deter-mines to "find/Strength in what remains". He has only "relinquished one delight" – he is still emotionally in touch with the more 'ordinary' aspects of Nature's "habitual sway". Indeed, he can still be moved to an extraordinary extent by the beauty of the world. So he ends his Ode on a positive, movingly reserved and quiet note:

To me the meanest flower that blows can give
Thoughts that do often lie too deep for tears.

"A host, of golden daffodils" *suddenly discovered on a solitary walk inspired Wordsworth's most famous poem. It is a beautifully simple expression of joy.*

Detail from a watercolour by Karen Armitage: Bridgeman Art Library

Enjoyment of Byron's and Keats' poetry does not depend on understanding all their classical references, but here are some explanations which might help.

DON JUAN
The Aeneid: Roman epic poem by Virgil
Ovid, Catullus: Roman love poets
Juvenal, Martial: Roman satirists
Banquo: in Shakespeare's *Macbeth*, he is murdered by Macbeth, whom he later haunts

ODE TO A NIGHTINGALE
Opiate: drug containing opium
Lethe: the Underworld River of Forgetfulness
Dryad: wood–nymph
Flora: goddess of flowers
Hippocrene: in Greek mythology, a fountain sacred to the Muses
Bacchus: god of wine
Pards: leopards
Poesy: art of poetry
Fay: fairy
Darkling: in the dark
Ruth: Old Testament heroine who lived in self-imposed exile

Coleridge
The Ancient Mariner

Coleridge was the disorganized genius of English Romantic poetry. Philosopher, critic, journalist and dramatist, he devoted relatively little time to poetry itself. And yet between 1797 and 1798 he created three of the greatest of all Romantic poems: *Kubla Khan, Christabel* and *The Rime of the Ancient Mariner. The Ancient Mariner* has a strange, haunting quality – its bizarre story, its weird remoteness, its strikingly vivid imagery and its simple, repetitive rhymes and rhythms remain with the reader like a half-remembered, half-understood dream.

The poem was written for Coleridge and Wordsworth's joint venture, the *Lyrical Ballads*, in which Coleridge was to write poems where 'the incidents and agents were to be, in part at least, supernatural; and the excellence aimed at was to consist in . . . the dramatic truth of such emotions, as would naturally accompany such situations, supposing them real'.

The plan of the poem began during a walk on the Quantock Hills with Wordsworth on 20 November 1797. The story itself was based on a dream experienced by Wordsworth's neighbour John Cruickshank, about a 'person suffering from a dire curse for the commission of some crime' and a 'skeleton ship with figures in it'. Added to these thoughts was Wordsworth's idea of a man who killed an albatross (a good omen) and was attacked by avenging spirits. Coleridge wove these elements together to create his unique, mysterious poem.

The Ancient Mariner is a masterpiece of

"Kubla Khan"
(above) One of Coleridge's three dream-like masterpieces, Kubla Khan *was – according to the poet – 'seen' in his head while he lay dreaming, having fallen asleep reading a book about the Khan (king) Kubla's palace and garden. When he woke, he wrote down the poem exactly as he remembered it – until a visitor interrupted him.*

spell-binding storytelling. We are hypnotized by the simple force of the language, with its rhythmic repetitions, its urgent tempo. The Mariner's compulsion to tell his tale is evoked immediately when he grasps the Wedding Guest's hand and blurts out "There was a ship". From that moment on, the Wedding Guest (and the reader) "cannot choose but hear his story".

Coleridge's sense of drama is obvious. The poem is packed with powerful visual images and sounds: the ice "mast high/Came floating by,/As green as emerald"; it "cracked and growled, and roared and howled". The strange landscape and stranger happenings are made real through such detailed physical descriptions. Colours are both realistic and symbolic. Red is used to liken the bride to a rose, and, in complete contrast – when the Mariner has committed his terrible, futile crime of shooting the albatross – it becomes the colour of a hellish "bloody sun, at noon".

This red sun hangs directly over the ship, which is becalmed:

"The Rime of the Ancient Mariner"
The long ballad of the Ancient Mariner, his needless slaughter of the innocent albatross and his subsequent nightmarish guilt, punishment and penance has the strange, surreal logic of a dream. It reveals Coleridge at the height of his genius.

Gustave Doré

Paul Bril: Fantastic Landscape. Johnny Van Haeften Gallery/Bridgeman Art Library

Day after day, day after day,
We stuck, nor breath nor motion;
As idle as a painted ship
Upon a painted ocean.

The water rots and "slimy things did crawl with legs/Upon the slimy sea". Tongues wither "at the root", lips are "baked black" – and the desperate crew hang the dead albatross round the Mariner's neck as a sign of his guilt.

A ghostly skeleton ship sails by, carrying two figures – Death and Life-in-Death – who throw dice for the ship's crew. Life-in-Death wins the Mariner. Death must have won the rest of the crew, because one after another they fall to the deck, lifeless. Only the Mariner remains. He closes his eyes, trying to escape from the "rotting sea", and the "rotting deck" where "the dead men lay":

I closed my eyes, and kept them close,
And the balls like pulses beat;

The spell begins to lift when the Mariner feels a spontaneous rush of love for the beautiful water-snakes in the moonlit sea. The desolate scene is transformed, and the Mariner at last arrives back on dry land. But he is ever afterwards haunted by the memory of his crime and is compelled to retell his "ghastly tale" over and over again.

In Coleridge's marginal notes, in which he summarizes and explains the action, he writes: "And ever and anon throughout his future life an agony constraineth him to travel from land to land. And to teach, by his own example, love and reverence to all things that God madeth and loveth." That is the poem's stated moral: but it is the poetic force of the Mariner's guilt for his inexplicable crime that haunts and lingers, making both Wedding Guest and reader "wiser" after hearing the strange tale.

"Christabel"
This mysterious poem tells the story of a medieval lady, Christabel, who is threatened by the evil spirit that haunts the body of "fair Geraldine".

Byron
Don Juan

'A work of boundless genius manifesting the most bitter and savage hatred of humanity, and then again penetrated with the most profound and tender love for mankind', was one German reviewer's response to *Don Juan*. Most English criticism was less favourable. 'Love – honour – patriotism – religion, are mentioned only to be scoffed at,' wrote one contemporary who saw Byron as a 'cool unconcerned fiend, laughing with detestable glee over the whole of the better and worse elements of which human life is composed'.

Byron initially said that 'Donny Jonny', as he called it, had no plan, but later argued that it had a strong moral line. It is a wide-ranging assault on the "kingdom of cant", exposing a catalogue of hypocrisy, pretentiousness and self-deceit.

Don Juan is a brilliant mix of satire, farce, blasphemy, passion and comment. The jokes are excellent, the rhymes ingenious, the tone conversational and infectiously high-spirited.

Byron chooses as his 'picaresque', wandering hero "our ancient friend/Don Juan", whose 'journey through life' is the story of the poem. Throughout the twelve cantos, the handsome young Spaniard engages in amorous exploits with various women, and travels from Spain to Greece, Turkey, Russia and England. But the story is only half of *Don Juan* – the author's comments are equally important. And although it is a free-wheeling poem, it is held together by Byron's dashing personality. He uses an unexpected, witty rhyme to puncture fine-sounding ideas and add irony and realism. Of Juan's education, he writes –

He learn'd the arts of riding, fencing, gunnery
And how to scale a fortress – or a nunnery.

We learn about the hypocrisy of society marriages and manners. But the poem also makes a powerful literary statement. For Byron had almost as much in common with the 18th-century Augustan satirists as with his Romantic contemporaries, whose verse he

Don Juan *has his first amorous adventure with Julia. At the end of the first canto their secret is revealed when Julia's husband "stumbled o'er a pair of shoes" in her bedroom. Juan is forced to flee Spain and travels to new lands, and new women.*

considered overblown, egotistical and not a little ridiculous. In stanzas XC-XCIII, Wordsworth and Coleridge receive irresistibly clever put-downs, as Byron describes Juan in the throes of first love, lying around in forests where "poets find materials for their books", which we can read –

So that their plan and prosody are eligible
Unless, like Wordsworth, they prove unintelligible.

Juan continues his "self-communion with his own high soul", turning, "without perceiving his condition/Like Coleridge, into a metaphysician." He then bends his lovelorn thoughts to the wonders of Nature and the mysteries of the universe. Byron comments:

If you think 'twas philosophy that this did,
I can't help thinking puberty assisted.

Byron is mocking himself as well as the other Romantics: like them, he had dreams and

"Childe Harold's Pilgrimage"
Byron's early masterpiece tells of the adventures and reflections of Childe Harold, a wandering hero who in many ways anticipates Don Juan. Both these characters are often viewed as psychological portraits of Byron – as this illustration from Childe Harold *implies.*

Mary Evans Picture Library

ideals, but was also a realist. As he himself said, *Don Juan* 'is a little quietly facetious about everything.'

At the outset, he upsets the orthodox idea of an epic poem. "I want [lack] a hero", he confesses, and in so doing is already flouting convention, for an epic without a hero was unheard-of.

Juan himself is nothing like the archetypal seducer we might expect; he enters as "A little curly-headed, good-for-nothing". At 16 he falls in love with his mother's friend Donna Julia, who "was married, charming, chaste, and twenty three" – with a 50-year-old husband. Julia loves Juan, but tries to keep the affair platonic (non-sexual). After an attack on Plato and his "confounded fantasies", Byron moves Juan and Julia closer and closer to the "immense" precipice:

A little still she strove, and much repented,
And whispering 'I will ne'er consent' – consented.

Their 'Fall' – the consummation of their passion – seems inevitable, especially, comments Byron, in a hot country like Spain:

What men call gallantry, and gods adultery,
Is much more common where the climate's sultry.

As the canto continues, the lovers are discovered in a farcical scene, and Juan is forced to flee. Julia sends him a beautifully touching letter, he swears never-ending loyalty, but she will soon be forgotten. The wise-cracking humour of Don Juan heightens its serious message. But Byron's contemporaries could not see beyond irreverence. Still, as Byron said 'If people won't discover the moral, that is their fault, not mine.'

Byronic heroes

Byron himself, as much as his characters, was the model for what became known as the 'Byronic hero' – a melancholy rebel like Harold, a Romantic outcast like Don Juan, 'a man, proud, moody, cynical with defiance on his brow . . . yet capable of deep and strong affection'.

Aivazovsky: Farewell to the Black Sea. Fine Art Photographic Library

Shelley
The Mask of Anarchy

Cruikshank. Mansell Collection

I met murder on the way —
He had a face like Castlereagh —
Very smooth he looked, yet grim;
Seven blood-hounds followed him:

A terrifying procession of allegorical figures followed Murder (Castlereagh, the Foreign Secretary): Fraud (Lord Eldon, Lord Chancellor), Hypocrisy (Lord Sidmouth, Home Secretary), and various bishops and lawyers.

Shelley's fury gives rise to short, vivid lines and violent images. Those responsible for the savagery are pictured as blood-hounds chewing on human hearts, and knocking out children's brains.

Last in the "ghastly masquerade" came "Anarchy" (misgovernment), riding "On a white horse, splashed with blood", with a mark on his brow proclaiming "I am GOD, AND KING, AND LAW". The procession, the "triumph of Anarchy", which hires murderers for wages of "glory, and blood, and gold", passes through England, destroying, "Tearing up, and trampling down". It is a grim world, complete with a skeleton bowing and grinning.

But Anarchy's drive forward is halted by a "manic maid" called Hope. Between these two figures a weird mist, then vapour, then storm clouds arise. Finally an armoured figure takes shape and knocks Anarchy from his horse. Death's riderless horse "with his hoofs

S helley was, more than any other Romantic poet, fired by ideas and ideals rather than by personal experience. But his expression of these ideals gains its power from the emotional intensity of his belief. *The Mask of Anarchy* is an unforgettable, angry attack on oppression, and a stirring call to stand together and destroy tyranny by passive, massed strength.

Shelley spent the late summer of 1819 reading in Florence. But his repose was shattered when a shipment of papers arrived with news from England. A crowd of 60,000 unarmed demonstrators had gathered on the outskirts of Manchester for an anti-Government rally. The local magistrate called in the Yeomanry to arrest the main speaker and disperse the crowd. Unintentionally, they knocked down a woman and trampled her child to death. The furious crowd surged forward, hemming in the army. Swords raised, the mounted Hussars rode in to support their colleagues, leaving 11 people dead and 420 badly injured. The incident became known as the Peterloo Massacre. Shelley was outraged, and retaliated with one of the greatest political protest poems in the language.

The Mask of Anarchy begins with a brilliant satirical onslaught against Government ministers. With startling directness, Shelley punches home his initial statement of hatred for the politicians behind that slaughter:

"The Mask of Anarchy"
This angry response to news of the 'Peterloo Massacre' at Manchester in 1819 was so powerful that it could not be published until 1832, ten years after Shelley's death. The 'Mask' refers to a procession or masquerade of the politicians whom Shelley blames for the massacre and the oppression of the masses whom he calls upon to "Rise like lions after slumber/In unvanquishable number."

"Ode to the West Wind"
Written in a wood outside Florence, Shelley's famous ode evokes the power and energy of the autumn wind, which threatens winter yet also holds the promise of spring.

Dahl: Birch Tree in a Storm. Bergen. Billedgalleri, Norway

"To a Skylark"
(left) The soaring song of an unseen skylark heard "In the golden lightning/Of the sunken sun" inspired Shelley's most famous lyrical poem. He asks the bird to share the secret of its divine bliss, so that he might express such joy in words.

"Adonais"
Shelley's elegy on the death of Keats (pictured on his deathbed, below) takes its name from the Greek god of beauty. It does not express personal sorrow, but is a magnificent contemplation of the tragically early loss to the world of such a noble spirit.

did grind/To dust the murderers thronged behind". The innocent get their revenge.

Hope explains to the crowd the meaning of slavery and of Freedom, and tells them that their guiding lights should be "Science, Poetry and Thought".

Then comes the rallying call for the crowd to stand up for its rights and demonstrate. The language, as ever, is simple, direct and highly charged.

> '*Let a vast assembly be,*
> *And with great solemnity*
> *Declare with measured words that ye*
> *Are, as God had made ye, free –*'

The commas in the last line give a final, conclusive emphasis to the word "free". Shelley is advocating passive, not violent resistance. They must "Stand . . . calm and resolute", even against the wheeling and flashing scimitars, the slashing, stabbing tyrants. Determinedly peaceful behaviour is their best weapon and a moral example that will force the troops to "return with shame/To the place from which they came."

Shelley's tone changes dramatically in the last three stanzas. Stoicism is replaced by a build-up to tremendous triumph. The crowd's words will ring "through each heart and brain". The poem's conclusion could even be a chant of demonstrators: "Ye are many – they are few."

This was such powerful writing that it could not be published in Shelley's lifetime. Under the law it was a libel, and at a time of political unrest and prosecutions of the 'free' press, its publisher was liable to imprisonment.

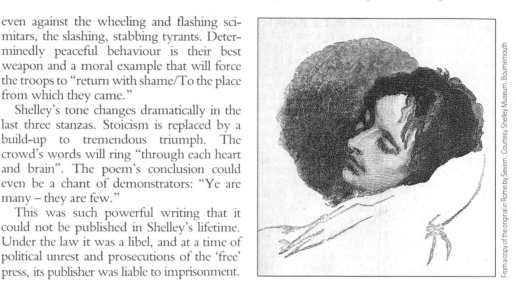

❦ *Keats* ❦
Ode to a Nightingale

Keats' unique poetic gift blossomed into maturity when he was just 23 years old, in what has become known as his 'Great Year', 1818-1819. He wrote his famous sequence of five Odes within about three weeks in late April and May 1819. One central theme of the Odes is the search for beauty and permanence amid the inevitable pain and transience of human existence.

In *Ode to a Nightingale*, Keats begins by hoping to achieve a mystic union with the nightingale's song – for him a symbol of immortality. He thinks he can attain this union first through wine, then poetry, and then death. But finally he recognizes that his desire to escape from the world is futile – that death is part of the process of life.

The poem itself was written rapidly – within a few hours. His friend John Brown described its composition: 'In the spring of 1819 a nightingale had built her nest near my house. Keats felt a tranquil and continual joy in her song; and one morning he took his chair . . . to the grass-plot under a plum tree, where he sat for two or three hours. When he came into the house, I perceived he had some scraps of paper in his hand, and these he was quietly thrusting behind some books . . . those scraps . . . contained his poetic feeling on the song of our nightingale.'

For a poem inspired by the joy of hearing the nightingale's song, the first lines may seem surprising:

> *My heart aches, and a drowsy numbness pains*
> *My sense, as though of hemlock I had drunk,*
> *Or emptied some dull opiate to the drains*

But Keats seems to be saying that his acute awareness of the bird's "Happiness" has triggered a state of heavy, almost drugged languor. He yearns to fuse with the freshness and beauty of the nightingale's song, and in the second stanza calls for the warmth and intoxication of wine to bring him nearer to the bird. The sensuous image of a beaker full of wine –

Holman Hunt: Laing Art Gallery, Tyne & Wear County Council Museum

Millais. Courtesy Her Majesty Queen Elizabeth, the Queen Mother

"The Eve of St Agnes"

(above) Madeline prepares for sleep on St Agnes' Eve, when legend says maidens dream of their future love. Unknown to her, she is not alone. She wakes to find her dream real: her lover is with her.

"Isabella"

(above) Though poignant and beautiful, Isabella *displays the morbid sentimentality that mars Keats' early work. Isabella is seen here mourning over a pot of basil – which contains the head of her murdered lover.*

"Ode to a Nightingale"

(left) This painting depicts Keats listening to the nightingale. Ode to a Nightingale *was probably the second of the 'Spring Odes' of 1819 – the others being 'Psyche', 'Grecian Urn', 'Melancholy', and 'Indolence'. In September, he wrote his final great Ode, To Autumn, the climax of the Spring sequence, which celebrates life's natural cycle.*

With beaded bubbles winking at the brim
And purple stained mouth;

suggests jollity and positive sensuous pleasure. But then the real, negative reason for Keats' desire to escape with the nightingale begins to assert itself:

That I might drink, and leave the world unseen,
And with thee fade away into the forest dim:

He wants to escape from the real world of pain, decay and death. The youth who "grows pale, and spectre-thin, and dies" is Keats' beloved brother Tom.

In the fourth stanza the poet claims that he will use "Poesy" (a deliberately affected name for poetry), not wine to enter the beautiful world of the nightingale's song.

Already with thee! Tender is the night,
And haply the Queen-Moon is on her throne
Cluster'd around by all her starry Fays;

He pretends that he has achieved his union, but the artificial, self-consciously 'poetic' language reveals that this is an illusion. The poet stops pretending, and becomes aware that he is in the real world, in the semi-darkness beneath the trees. He uses his imagination to "guess" at the flowers that surround him:

I cannot see what flowers are at my feet,
Nor what soft incense hangs upon the boughs,
But, in embalmed darkness, guess each sweet
Wherewith the seasonal month endows
The grass, the thicket, and the fruit-tree wild;

His sensuous response to the physical world has much more substance and real beauty than the artifice of 'Poesy'. But thinking of spring flowers, he remembers the process of Nature: violets are 'Fast fading'. Musing about the changing seasons leads him to thoughts of death. He mocks his own indulgent fantasies about "easeful Death", but is still drawn to the idea of leaving behind pain in the ultimate mystical union with Nature. But the poet realizes that this is another vain fantasy. Dying would not achieve an immortal union with the bird's music: he would simply hear the "full-throated" song no longer – and it would become his requiem.

Keats begins the 7th stanza by strenuously asserting the immortality of the nightingale's song (not the nightingale itself), which has been heard since ancient days. He imagines Biblical characters listening, then moves further into a fanciful past where the nightingale's music floats into "magic casements . . . in faery lands forlorn".

This over-indulgence brings the poet back to his senses, to the here and now. The nightingale's song begins to fade – it has become merely a "plaintive anthem" which dies away and is "buried deep/In the next valley glades", not a symbol of immortality.

Keats is left wondering whether his experience has been meaningful, or deceptive fantasy. But although the ending is ambiguous, the gentle fading of the nightingale's song is so beautifully described that it becomes a powerful argument for accepting that joy and decay should not be separated and that human happiness is richer for its fragility.

Romanticism

Poets of vision and revolution, the Romantics rejected the values of 18th-century rationalists and revelled in the power of the Imagination – their key to the mysteries of the universe.

Many of the revolutionary characteristics of Romanticism are taken for granted today; and, like most historical phenomena, the Romantic Movement can only be understood in terms of what came before. It represented a violent reaction to the political, social, intellectual and artistic climate of the 18th century, and occurred – by no coincidence – against the setting of the French Revolution. It was a parallel idealistic bid for freedom (in language) and represented a parallel shift in concerns and values. These concerns particularly affected the extraordinary group of poets who gave the Romantic Movement in England its substance and direction.

The French Revolution itself was a primary source of inspiration for the 'first generation' of Romantic poets: Wordsworth, Coleridge and Blake. It seemed to signal the victory of liberty over tyranny, and triggered a time of change when accepted norms were being questioned and tested.

While these poets were fired by political and social changes, the 'second generation' of Romantics – Byron, Shelley and Keats – reacted against the absence of them. They grew up in a society in which privilege and oppression had been reasserted by a series of Tory governments. Shelley and Byron in particular applied their art to satirizing leading political figures, and expressing their outrage at the state of the Nation.

Apart from responding to external, political changes, Romanticism reflected an even more fundamental, internal revolution – a radical change in attitude towards the value of personal human experience. The 17th and early 18th centuries had been a time of scientific discovery, an age when investigation and analysis were seen as the tools of enlightenment, and when human beings were primarily valued as citizens who played their 'correct' roles in society.

If the 18th century saw itself as the Age of Reason, the Romantic era was the Age of Emotion. The Romantics were interested in feelings, not facts. They emphasized passion and atmosphere over precision and argument. All good poetry, wrote Wordsworth, 'is the spontaneous overflow of personal feelings'. The Romantic era was an age of grand gestures and rhetorical flourishes, an age when defiance was more fashionable than decorum.

There were three major areas in which Romantic writers differed markedly from

their immediate predecessors: in their attitudes to the Individual, to Imagination, and to Nature.

Human beings were seen by the Romantics as individuals rather than members of society – individuals whose emotional responses were more important than their rational ones. Their real links were with Nature rather than the artificiality of urban, social existence, and they did not accept that established religious ideas and social rules were necessarily 'the truth'. Instead they sought a freer concept of truth based on individual experience and – most importantly – the Imagination.

Revolutionary inspiration
(left) The French Revolution focused some of the radical ideas and ideals of the Romantic movement. It represented an attempt to overthrow a system of oppression and feudal privilege and allow the common people their freedom and dignity.

Grimshaw: River Landscape. Roy Miles Gallery. Bridgeman Art Library

Gustave Doré

Bertaux: Taking of the Tuileries Palace. Musée de Versailles/Bridgeman Art Library

Return to Nature
(left) For the Romantics, cities spelt confusion, corruption and false values, and it was only in Nature – in its various moods, from gentle to wild and sublime – that Truth and Inspiration could be found. A magnificent mountain scene (below) could bring about an ecstatic vision, such as Wordsworth described in The Prelude*: "And I have felt/A presence that disturbs me with the joy/Of elevated thoughts; a sense sublime . . ."*

Supernatural images
The Romantics were intent on capturing fleeting images, which might have been inspired by dreams, drugs or simply unrestrained reverie. In writing The Rime of the Ancient Mariner *(left), Coleridge maintained that his rational mind was held in abeyance, allowing his psyche to conjure up obsessions, forebodings and hallucinations that lie just below the surface of consciousness.*

Milner: An Alpine Lake. Private Collection. Bridgeman Art Library

Key Dates

1757 William Blake born in London

1770 William Wordsworth born at Cockermouth, Cumbria

1772 Samuel Taylor Coleridge born at Ottery St Mary, Devon

1783 Britain defeated in American War of Independence

1788 George Gordon Byron born in London

1789 French Revolution begins. Blake's *Songs of Innocence* published

1790 Wordsworth in France

1792 Percy Bysshe Shelley born at Field Place, Sussex. France becomes a republic

1793 Britain at war with France (1793–1802; 1803–15)

1794 Blake's *Songs of Experience* published

1795 John Keats born in London

1797 Coleridge writes *Kubla Khan*

1797–98 Wordsworth and Coleridge working together in Somerset

1798 *Lyrical Ballads* published

1800–08 Wordsworth at Dove Cottage

1802 Wordsworth marries Mary Hutchinson

1804 Napoleon becomes Emperor of France

1805 Nelson victorious at Trafalgar, Napoleon at Austerlitz. Wordsworth finishes *The Prelude*

1809 Byron's *English Bards and Scotch Reviewers*

1811 Shelley's *The Necessity of Atheism*. Shelley sent down from Oxford

1812 *Childe Harold* makes Byron famous

1813 Wordsworth becomes Distributor of Stamps and moves to Rydal Mount. Jane Austen's *Pride and Prejudice* published

1814 Fall of Napoleon. Shelley elopes with Mary Godwin. Scott's *Waverley* published

1815 Napoleon returns from Elba and is defeated at Waterloo. Byron marries Annabella Milbanke

1816 Byron separates from his wife and leaves England. Friendship with Shelley begins

1817 Coleridge's *Biographia Literaria* published

1818 Mary Shelley's *Frankenstein*, and Keats' *Endymion* published

1818–19 Keats' 'Great Year' of creativity

1819 Byron meets Countess Guiccioli; first two cantos of *Don Juan* published. Shelley writes *The Mask of Anarchy*

1821 Keats dies in Rome. Shelley writes *Adonais* in his memory. Napoleon dies on St Helena

1822 Wordsworth's *Guide to the Lakes*. Shelley drowned in the Bay of Spezia

1824 Death of Byron at Missolonghi

1827 Death of Blake

1829 Greece wins independence

1834 Coleridge dies

1843 Wordsworth becomes Poet Laureate

1850 Death of Wordsworth. *The Prelude* published

'I am certain of nothing but the holiness of the Heart's affections, and the truth of Imagination', wrote Keats. And indeed, despite their individual differences, all the Romantic poets (except, perhaps, for Byron) shared this belief in the importance of Imagination. It was the key to their poetry, to their understanding of the meaning of things, and to their very existence. Without Imagination, they were nothing; with it they could glimpse the innermost secrets of the Universe.

In his *Prophetic Books,* William Blake talked of the need to 'cast aside from Poetry all that is not Inspiration'. His chief complaint about his Royal Academy training was that 'copying nature deadened the force of my imagination'; it is noticeable that his own drawings are nearly always symbolic and very rarely strictly representational. And in Coleridge's *The Ancient Mariner, Christabel* and *Kubla Khan,* the poetic utterance seems to belong less to the domain of reason than to that of dream or nightmare.

A dream-like atmosphere is common to a number of great works of Romanticism. Coleridge's particular poetic visions were undoubtedly stimulated by his addiction to opium – a drug that seemed for a while to free the mind from its chains. The hallucinatory effect of opium and laudanum (which were taken medicinally in the 19th century) can often be glimpsed in the imagery of Romantic poems such as Keats' *Ode to a Nightingale* and *Ode on Melancholy.* Thomas De Quincey's book *Confessions of an English Opium Eater* was partly the self-apology of an addict, and partly a glorification of the powers of the Imagination.

The Romantics' fascination with Imagination might also account for another of their concerns – the world of childhood. To them, children had the capacity to see things more

Solitary hero
Inspired by a Thomas Gray poem, John Martin's
The Bard expresses the Romantic idea of the poet.
High on a cliff-top, the solitary bard stands firm,
shouting defiance at the soldiers below.

WILLIAM BLAKE

Born in London in 1757, William Blake was in many ways the quintessential Romantic. He was a radical, a visionary and he had a completely original, personal way of viewing the world and of expressing that view. With no orthodox education, he was nevertheless extremely well-read, having nurtured himself on such works as the Bible and the writings of Dante, Shakespeare and Milton.

During his lifetime he earned his living as an engraver. His poems, which he had been writing since childhood, and his paintings received little attention until after his death. Today, however, he is recognized as a total artist - poet, painter, engraver and printer.

Blake intentionally set himself up against what he saw as the mechanistic thought-processes of 'Enlightenment' philosophers and scientists like John Locke and Isaac Newton. In extolling a world of reason, they seemed to rob the universe of its majesty and mystery. To Blake, instead, humans' 'invisible' nature - their imagination - was proof of the existence of God; indeed it was a manifestation of God in the human soul.

Blake's best and most accessible poems are *Songs of Innocence*, which celebrate childhood joy and spontaneity, and *Songs of Experience*, which offer a deeper study of maturity and deal with corruption and social injustice.

Portrait by Thomas Phillips. National Portrait Gallery

Blake's symbols
In writing The Sick Rose *(below), one of his* Songs of Experience, *Blake (left) explored the subtle suggestiveness of Romantic poetry. The rose has been variously interpreted as symbolizing love, the human soul, the world, or woman; the worm, by contrast, has been seen as the flesh, the devil, corruption or man. While the vocabulary Blake uses is precise and clear, the symbolism is dark, mysterious, resonant – and open to individual interpretation.*

Fotomas Index

John Martin: The Bard. Laing Art Gallery, Tyne & Wear County Council Museum

Tate Gallery

Against rationalism
In portraying Sir Isaac Newton (left) under water (the symbol of materialism), Blake showed his hatred of scientific rationalism. For him as for the other Romantics, Newton was the enemy of life, stripping it of its majesty by reducing it to mechanical formulae.

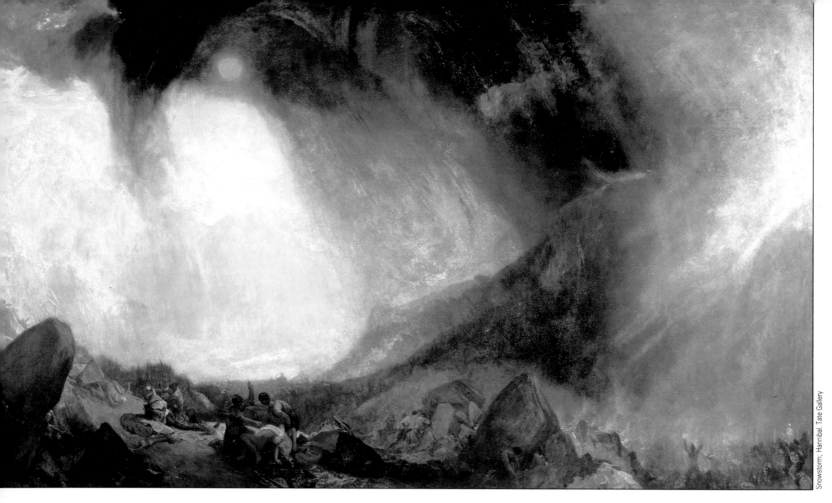

English Romantic art

Like the Romantic poets, Romantic painters set out to experience the variety of Nature. Joseph Turner once had himself tied to a ship's mast in order to be able to paint the full onslaught of a storm.

clearly than adults did. As Coleridge once stated, 'The Poet is the one who carries the simplicity of childhood into the powers of manhood; who, with a soul unsubdued by habit, unshackled by custom, contemplates all things with the freshness and wonder of a child.' Certainly Blake's *Songs of Innocence* and Wordsworth's poems *The Prelude* and *Tintern Abbey* value the freshness and immediacy of child-like intuition over the clumsier results of adult reasoning and experience.

A favourite subject of Romantic poetry was the poet himself. It was not a period of impersonal commentary, but was characterized by epics of either overt or disguised autobiography, such as Wordsworth's *The Prelude* or Byron's *Don Juan* or Odes such as those of Shelley and Keats. In these, the poetry distilled and expressed the mystical links the poet felt with the world as he experienced it. The Romantic period also included expression of obscure personal mythology, as in the later works of Blake.

For the Romantic artist, the individual was a being of infinite potential. Yet the artist also had a vision of himself as an outsider. Wordsworth's and Coleridge's most memorable poems are about solitude, and their most memorable characters, such as Coleridge's Ancient Mariner and Byron's Childe Harold, are isolated figures who seem not to have a natural place in the realm of ordinary society.

The Romantics saw themselves as rebels against established modes of thought, both artistic and political. Blake was not merely contemptuous of the traditional training he received at the Royal Academy of Arts; politically, his ideas were so extreme that on one occasion they were thought to be treasonable. Shelley was expelled from University College, Oxford, for his co-authorship of a deliberately provocative pamphlet, *The Necessity of Atheism.* And Byron's scandalous and allegedly incestuous private life shocked the conventional moral standards of the time and forced him into exile.

INSPIRATION IN NATURE

One of the qualities which set the Romantics apart from earlier poets was their attitude to Nature. In Nature they saw beauty, and out of beauty came inspiration. They undoubtedly reacted against an increasingly industrialized age and rejected the degrading and dehumanizing aspects of mechanization.

The Romantics' attitude to Nature was also a reaction against what they saw as the arrogant rationality of the previous age, and an attempt on their part to restore a sense of magic and wonder to human responses. Coleridge states this view when he describes Wordsworth's poetic aims in his *Biographia Literaria.* These were 'to excite a feeling analogous to the supernatural, by awakening the Mind's attention from the lethargy of custom and directing it to the loveliness and the wonders of the world before us.' Wordsworth's own lines in his poem *The*

Tables Turned perfectly captures the Romantic attitude to the mysterious beauty of Nature:

> *Sweet is the lore which Nature brings;*
> *Our meddling intellect*
> *Misshapes the beauteous form of things:*
> *We murder to dissect.*

Each Romantic poet tended to have his own individual views on Nature. For Wordsworth, Nature's inspiration provided sufficient subject-matter in itself. Coleridge habitually equated Nature with moral qualities. In *The Ancient Mariner,* Nature behaves throughout as a moral force, with drought, for example, symbolizing the Mariner's spiritual aridity, the rain his regeneration, the sun acting as an agent of punishment and the moon as one of redemption.

Other Romantics used Nature as a means of discussing their personal crises. For example, Keats' *Ode to a Nightingale* and Shelley's *Ode to the West Wind* are both as much about the problems of artistic creativity as about the wonders of Nature.

A significant fact is that the term 'Romantic' was not applied to any of these poets during their lifetime, either by others or by themselves. The importance of this is that they were not consciously following any school of thought and certainly not concerned to prove any particular theory. None of the famous critical texts of the period – Wordsworth's *Advertisement and Preface* to the *Lyrical Ballads,* Coleridge's *Biographia Literaria,* Shelley's *Defence of Poetry* – can really be seen as manifestoes of the Romantic movement. The essence of Romanticism is in the eloquence and fervour of the poems themselves.

THE WAR POETS

Brooke • Sassoon • Owen • Rosenberg

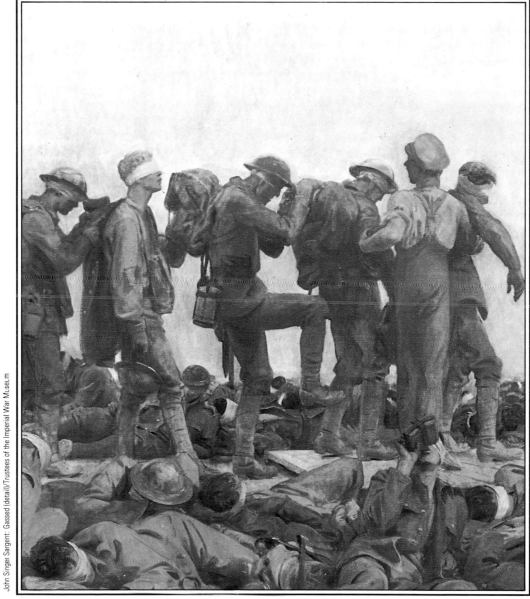

In prospect, World War I seemed like a great adventure: the patriotic vision of glory painted by Rupert Brooke captures that pre-War euphoria. But the adventure's descent into the most terrible slaughter shattered men's beliefs and optimism. Owen lamented while Sassoon raged and Rosenberg recorded, with stark concision, the filthy ordeal. Their works, and the other poetry featured here, document the deception, disillusion and destruction of a generation.

RUPERT BROOKE

→ 1887–1915 ←

Fired with patriotic idealism, Rupert Brooke epitomized the promise of golden youth. He died in 1915, before he had the chance to realize the true horrors of the war.

Rupert Brooke was the first and most famous of the War Poets – although, paradoxically, he had almost no first-hand experience of war. His sonnets, like no other poems, evoked the spirit of patriotic self-sacrifice with which England's young men answered the call to arms. And Brooke himself, 'the handsomest young man in England', came to symbolize an entire generation – golden, gifted and doomed.

Rupert Chawner Brooke was born on 3 August 1887 at Rugby. His father was a housemaster at Rugby public (private) school, where Brooke was a pupil until, in 1906, he won a classical scholarship to King's College, Cambridge.

At Cambridge he became an enthusiastic amateur actor, founded a club called the Carbonari and took an active part in the University branch of the socialist Fabian Society. It was here, too, that his schoolboy knack of writing verses developed into a vocation.

Surrounded by friends, Brooke delighted in life at Cambridge. Even after taking his degree in 1909, he lived in essentially the same fashion for several years more, settling with his mother at Grantchester, not far from Cambridge.

In 1911 the idyll was shattered by an emotional entanglement. Brooke became overpoweringly attracted to 'Ka' (Katherine) Cox, a young Cambridge Fabian, even though he knew that she was already involved with another man. After a painful triangular confrontation he came close to a nervous breakdown and fled abroad, staying in Berlin and Munich. Ka Cox later joined him in Munich, but the arrangement was not a success. They parted, leaving Brooke deeply scarred.

His state of mind at the time is reflected in a

Glittering gifts
Blessed with most earthly advantages – a sensitive mind, physical beauty, charismatic charm and social status – Rupert Brooke looked on war as the ultimate opportunity to express his personal valour and manliness.

Pre-War idyll
The year (1909) that Brooke was pictured (below left) picnicking on a warm summer's day, he graduated from King's College, Cambridge (below). Brooke continued to enjoy Cambridge life until an unhappy love affair made him seek solace in travel.

number of poems including the astonishingly venomous *Jealousy.* Yet in Berlin, apparently despairing, he also wrote the most famous of his pre-war poems – *Grantchester* – a partly-sentimental, partly-self-mocking work which now enshrines the myth of a happy, sunlit England before the First World War. Late in 1911, these and other poems appeared in his first published collection.

Among those who recognized in Brooke a new voice in English poetry was Edward Marsh, Winston Churchill's private secretary, who was

National Portrait Gallery, London

Mary Evans Picture Library

By permission of the Provost and Scholars of King's College, Cambridge

also an outstanding patron of the arts. Marsh gave a prominent place to Brooke's work in his *Georgian Poetry* anthologies, which largely shaped public taste from 1912 onwards. Brooke was now drawn increasingly into London society, where new friends, and a relationship with the actress Cathleen Nesbitt, helped to heal his wounds. Then in 1913 he was commissioned to write a series of travel articles by the *Westminster Gazette,* and spent a year in the United States, Canada and the South Sea Islands. Like so many Europeans he was enchanted by Tahiti – and particularly by a Tahitian girl named Taatamata. One of his finest poems, *Tiare Tahiti,* was inspired by his experiences there.

Within a few months of Brooke's return to England, the First World War had broken out. He volunteered, was commissioned in the Royal Naval Division and in October 1914 took part in the unsuccessful attempt to relieve Antwerp – his only direct experience of warfare. On his return, while training at Blandford, he wrote the five *1914 Sonnets. Peace,* beginning "Now, God be thanked Who has matched us with His hour", expressed a feeling, common among young men of his class, that the war was a supreme and welcome test. Another poem, *The Soldier,* is the most famous of all, prophetic of his own and many other deaths in "a foreign field".

At the end of February 1915, Brooke sailed with the Hood Battalion on the *Grantully Castle* for the Dardanelles. The ship put in at Port Said, where Sir Ian Hamilton offered Brooke a post on his staff there. He refused, and sailed with the ship. While apparently recovering from sunstroke and a sore on his lip, he was suddenly taken seriously ill. Diagnosed as suffering from acute blood poisoning, he was transferred to a French hospital ship, and died on 23 April 1915. He was buried in an olive grove on the Greek island of Skyros, his friends covering his grave with broken pieces of marble. Within weeks, these friends too would die, at Gallipoli.

During his absence, Brooke had become famous in England with the publication of his sonnets, one of which was read out in St Paul's Cathedral on Easter Sunday, 1915. When the news of his death arrived, obituaries by Churchill, Marsh and others mourned and praised him as a representative of England's glorious, high-hearted youth; and Rupert Brooke passed into legend.

"Some corner of a foreign field . . ."
Turning down a 'safe' job at Port Said (below), Brooke sailed with his men towards Gallipoli. But he was never to arrive. He had already contracted blood poisoning, and died on St George's Day, 1915. His friends buried him beneath the Greek sunshine, in an olive grove on the island of Skyros (right).

SIEGFRIED SASSOON

✦ 1886-1967 ✦

A hero of the war, Sassoon was also one of its most savage critics, using his honoured status and powerful poetic voice to shock the Establishment out of its complacency.

During the First World War, Siegfried Sassoon was the perfect gentleman–officer, worshipped by his men and decorated for outstanding valour. His status as a hero made his condemnation of the war all the more embarrassing for the authorities, who preferred to silence rather than confront him. In his poems, however, Sassoon gave forceful, scathing expression to the disillusionment that was increasingly felt by fighting men.

Siegfried Loraine Sassoon was born on 8 September 1886 at Weirleigh, near Paddock Wood in Kent. His father left the family when Sassoon was

A dashing hero
(right) Handsome, wealthy and a passionate sportsman, Sassoon rushed to be part of the Great Adventure in 1914. He was worshipped by his Yeoman troops for his reckless bravery, and awarded military honours. But probably his bravest stand was against the bigotry of the warmongers.

Glyn Philpot: Portrait of Sassoon, Fitzwilliam Museum, Cambridge

E. S. A. Douglas: Full Cry/Fine Art Photographic Library

a child, and he was brought up by his mother in a comfortable, cultivated but over-protective environment. After schooling at Marlborough College, he spent only four terms in 1905-6 at Clare College, Cambridge.

The next eight years were spent mainly at home, indulging his passion for hunting and playing cricket. On the surface, Sassoon appeared to be a rather ordinary country gentleman; his poetry – privately printed in small editions – showed some talent but seemed unlikely to develop beyond pleasant amateurism. He himself began to feel worried that 'my life was being wasted on sport and minor poetry'.

Sassoon's reaction to the outbreak of war on 4 August 1914 was predictably conventional; the following day he enlisted as a cavalry trooper in the Sussex Yeomanry. In May 1915 he transferred to the infantry, taking a commission in the Royal Welch Fusiliers, and he was posted to France in

November 1915. He soon showed himself to be a recklessly brave officer, and, according to Robert Graves, was nicknamed 'Mad Jack' by his men. In June 1916 he was awarded the Military Cross for bringing a wounded man back to the British lines under heavy fire, and for another exploit he was recommended for the Victoria Cross.

Ironically, the war gave Sassoon the motivation and the subject he needed to become a real poet. Until 1916, his verse described, rather than commented on, the harrowing experience of war. But in that year he discovered an unexpected talent for epigrammatic, harshly satirical writing that expressed his outrage at the carnage he was forced to witness. His verses savaged the warmongering of ignorant civilians and the complacent inhumanity of the generals, who sacrificed young lives by the hundred thousand. Sassoon also painted a dis-

Fox-hunting man at the Front
Sassoon's Memoirs of a Fox-Hunting Man *portrays his youth as a leisurely round of sports; but war changed all that. Bitter disillusion awaited in France, where chivalric ideals drowned in mud and blood. Despite his hatred of the war, Sassoon conscientiously returned to the battlefield after recovering from wounds, and served in both Palestine (right) and again in France.*

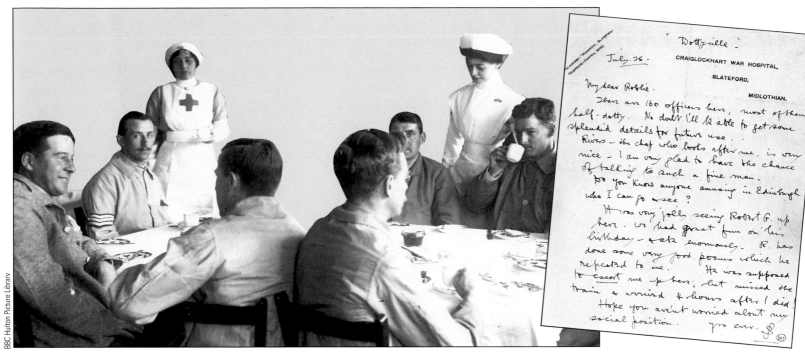

Outspoken poet

Like many wounded soldiers (above), Sassoon was temporarily sent home in 1917. Then he wrote A Soldier's Declaration *'against the political errors and insincerities for which the fighting men are being sacrificed'. Instead of court-martialling him, the authorities sent him to Craiglockhart Hospital. Here he kept a lively correspondence with – among others – Robert Ross (top right).*

concertingly 'unpatriotic' picture of the fighting man, longing to escape from the trenches to hospital, where "though his wound was healed and mended,/He hoped he'd get his leave extended."

Sassoon's wartime collections, *The Old Huntsman* (1917) and *Counter-Attack* (1918), were received with a mixture of respect and alarm by the literary establishment. *Counter-Attack* only just escaped suppression by the censors, but ultimately Sassoon's subversive attitudes were tolerated – at least in the world of poetry.

It was different when he tried to translate his ideas into action. The opportunity arose in April 1917, when he was wounded and sent back to England for treatment. In July he published *A Soldier's Declaration*, which announced that 'I am making this statement as an act of wilful defiance of military authority, because I believe that the war is being deliberately prolonged by those who have the power to end it.' Sassoon managed to get the *Declaration* read out in the House of Commons, and looked forward to a court-martial, believing that the attendant controversy might influence public opinion.

But the authorities were too shrewd to risk court-martialling a war hero. Instead, Sassoon was sent before a medical board, diagnosed as suffering from shell-shock, and sent to Craiglockhart War Hospital in Edinburgh. There he had his momentous encounter with fellow-patient Wilfred Owen, who was still finding his way as a poet. Owen had an immense admiration for Sassoon's work, and cherished his advice.

At Craiglockhart, Sassoon began to feel guilty at living in safety while others were fighting and dying. He persuaded his psychiatrist to let him return to the war, and served in Palestine and back in France before further wounds forced him to be put on indefinite sick leave.

After the war, Siegfried Sassoon had a long and distinguished literary career until his death on 1 September 1967. But he always wrote most vividly about his early years, notably in three semi-autobiographical works, *Memoirs of a Fox-Hunting Man* (1928), *Memoirs of an Infantry Officer* and *Sherston's Progress* (1936). Sassoon also published three volumes of straight autobiography including *Siegfried's Journey* (1945), describing his wartime experiences. These and his other works continue to be widely read. Nonetheless, it is on his achievement as a war poet that his high reputation ultimately rests.

A distinguished old man

Sassoon (below) was one of the few poets of the First World War who lived to see old age, and to fulfil his poetic promise. He died aged 80 in 1967.

WILFRED OWEN

➤ 1893-1918 ◆

Sensitive, shy, outstandingly brave in action, Owen focused his writing on 'the pity of war', to produce poems of unparalleled poignancy and compassion.

BBC Hulton Picture Library

Isolated from the literary society in which Rupert Brooke and Siegfried Sassoon moved so freely, Wilfred Owen struggled patiently to develop his gifts as a poet. His talent blossomed in 1917-18, after a chance wartime meeting with Sassoon. Like Sassoon, Owen was torn between revulsion against the war and a deep sense of responsibility to his men – a responsibility that eventually sent him back to the trenches, and to his death a week before the Armistice.

Wilfred Owen was born on 18 March 1893 at Oswestry in Shropshire. His originally prosperous middle-class family fell on hard times while he was still a child, and his educational career was confined to Birkenhead Institute and Shrewsbury Technical School. Nevertheless he was writing poetry in his teens, stimulated by his reading of the Romantics. Failing to win a scholarship to London University, he became a lay assistant to the vicar of Dunsden in Oxfordshire. But the

An inner power
Born and brought up in peaceful Shropshire (below), Wilfred Owen at 24 was in appearance 'provincial', but his poetry was far removed from the ordinary. His fellow officer and hero, Siegfried Sassoon, was his most generous and constructive critic, perceiving Owen's outstanding qualities, his 'inward power and integrity' – and maintaining that, 'had he lived longer, he would have produced poems of sustained grandeur . . .'

experience disillusioned Owen with institutionalized religion, and he left Dunsden in 1913, abandoning the idea of becoming a clergyman. In September that year, he struck out in a new direction, taking a job as a teacher of English at the Berlitz School in Bordeaux.

Overworked and badly paid, Owen had little time for poetry until August 1914, when he was hired as a private tutor by a kindly and affluent French family in the Pyrenees. Here he had his first

M. Crouse: Hadley near Shrewsbury/Fine Art Photographic Library

Scenes of France
Ironically, some of
Owen's happiest days
were spent in France
(above) as a tutor and
would-be man of letters,
before his involvement in
the war. But he attributed
his 'growing up' to being
'frozen alive with dead
men for comforters' on
such French battlefields
as Beaumont Hamel.

encounter with a literary man, the elderly poet and pacifist Laurent Tailhade. Apparently more preoccupied with literary ambition and financial problems than with the war, Owen continued to teach, even writing home that 'I feel my own life more precious and more dear in the presence of this deflowering of Europe.' But though his sentiments were already pacifist, the impulse to take his part in the conflict grew increasingly strong: in October 1915 he enlisted in the Artists' Rifles.

After undergoing training, Owen was commissioned as a 2nd Lieutenant, and on 1 January 1917 he joined the 2nd Manchester Regiment in France. The realities of water-logged trenches, barbed wire, bombardments and machine guns quickly destroyed any romantic notions he may have retained. He was briefly in hospital with concussion after a fall into a cellar, and then had a lucky escape when a shell landed just two yards from his head, flinging him into a hole which he occupied for several days, unnervingly close to the mangled corpse of a brother officer.

It soon became apparent that Owen had not escaped unscathed. When his speech became incoherent he was diagnosed as shell-shocked, repatriated in June 1917, and sent for observation and treatment to Craiglockhart War Hospital. He quickly became the editor of the hospital magazine *The Hydra*, in which he published *Song of Songs* – the first of his poems to appear in print.

Meanwhile Siegfried Sassoon had arrived at Craiglockhart. Owen nerved himself to approach

The Sitwells
Osbert and Edith Sitwell
(above) were at the centre
of a literary circle well
before the war began. The
poet Robert Ross
introduced Wilfred Owen
to them when Owen was
on summer leave in 1918,
and they later published
some of his greatest war
poems in their annual
anthology of modern
poetry, Wheels. It was
Edith who recognized
instantly the genius of
both Owen and Isaac
Rosenberg, and wrote in
1922, 'Rosenberg was one
of the two great poets
killed in the war, the other
being Wilfred Owen.'

the already famous – or notorious – poet, asking him to sign some copies of *The Old Huntsman*. 'Short, dark-haired, and shyly hesitant' – and also 'perceptibly provincial' – he made a good impression on Sassoon. When he was shown Owen's poems, Sassoon recognized their potential and became his new friend's literary mentor, urging him to prune his lush romantic style and write in a more direct, colloquial vein. Encouraged by Sassoon, and by Sassoon's friend Robert Graves, Owen wrote some of his finest, most angry and compassionate poems over the next few months. These included *Anthem for Doomed Youth*, *Disabled*, *Dulce et Decorum Est* and *Strange Meeting*.

When he left Craiglockhart, it was with introductions written by Sassoon that opened the doors of London literary society to him. He met H. G. Wells, Arnold Bennett and the Sitwells. One of his poems appeared in *The Nation* (his first national magazine publication), the Sitwells asked him to contribute to an anthology, and the publisher Heinemann offered to bring out a collection of his verse. It was for this that Owen wrote his famous preface, declaring that 'The Poetry is in the pity'.

Although his future now seemed so promising, Owen began to feel that he should leave his safe home posting and return to France. Declared fit in August 1918, he fought in the fierce action on the Beaurevoir-Fousomme line, and was awarded the Military Cross. Then, in the early hours of 4 November, leading his men across the Sambre Canal, Wilfred Owen fell under machine-gun fire.

ISAAC ROSENBERG
←1890-1918→

Unable to earn a living despite his various talents, Rosenberg volunteered to fight – against his principles. Recognition was to come to him only after his death.

National Portrait Gallery

A radically different figure from the officer-poets who served on the Western Front, Isaac Rosenberg was working class and fought in the ranks of the British Army as a private. Rosenberg's death in action was the final defeat in his bitter struggle to rise out of poverty and establish himself as a writer and artist. The full stature of his verse – so much less traditional in form and tone than his contemporaries' – was to

Self-portrait
Rosenberg painted this self-portrait in 1915. That year, he enlisted – despite his anti-war convictions – hoping that his mother would be given half his pay as a 'separation allowance'.

Isaac Rosenberg: Portrait of the artist's father. Carlisle Museum and Art Gallery

Emigrant Father
Fleeing military service in Russia, Barnett Rosenberg emigrated to England. Though a cultured man, respected at the synagogue, he, his wife and six children lived in severe poverty. Barnett was a pedlar, his wife a washerwoman and seamstress. At one time the family lived seven to a room, sustained only by the kinship of their equally poor neighbours, and by support from charitable organisations.

London's East End
No social advantages boosted Rosenberg's career as a poet or painter. He had only the support of his friends. The sector of London's East End (below) where he grew up was essentially Jewish, but he always maintained that he wanted to be an English rather than a Jewish poet. It was in painting that he made the breakthrough in his lifetime, becoming one of 'The Whitechapel Boys', the East End's wave of talented young artists.

established woman artist, Lily Delissa Joseph. She organized the financial support that in 1911 enabled Rosenberg to become a full-time student of art at the prestigious Slade School.

During his years at the Slade, Rosenberg made only slow progress as a painter. His poems remained unpublished until he borrowed £2 and paid a printer in the Mile End Road to produce a booklet containing the long poem *Night and Day* and nine other pieces. All 50 copies were given away, not sold. However, in November 1913 Rosenberg met Edward Marsh, who proved a generous patron; he bought a number of Rosenberg's paintings and drawings, though the unconventional nature of the poems made him uneasy.

After leaving the Slade in the Spring of 1914, Rosenberg became ill. To mend his weak lungs he sailed to Cape Town, where his sister and her husband had settled. Arriving in June 1914, he lec-

be generally acclaimed only after several decades.

Isaac Rosenberg, the son of Jewish immigrants from Lithuania (Russia) was born in Bristol on 25 November 1890. In 1897 the family moved to London's East End, and Rosenberg went to the local elementary school. There a sympathetic headmaster helped him to discover a talent for drawing; but when he reached 14 he had to leave school and go out to work.

Taken on as an apprentice by a Fleet Street engraving firm, Rosenberg found the work hard, mechanical and unhealthy. But his earnings did enable him to study art seriously at the evening classes held at Birkbeck College. Now, as later, he hoped to make a profitable career as an artist while also pursuing his other vocation – poetry.

At 20, Rosenberg left the engraver's, rejoicing that 'I'm free – free to do anything, hang myself or anything except work'. But, living at home on his dwindling savings, he failed to sell either his drawings or his writings. He was considering emigration when his luck suddenly turned. While copying a painting in the National Gallery, he met an

Museum of London

tured on art, painted portraits and had a number of his poems published in magazines. But although this seems to have been the happiest and most successful period in Rosenberg's life, he missed London and in February 1915 returned home.

Wartime London had little use for Rosenberg's talents, and when he again published a small collection of poems – *Youth* – it sold only ten copies. Despondent and desperate, he increasingly saw enlistment as the answer to his problems, despite his conviction that 'Nothing can justify war'. Like many others he felt that in fighting he would, somehow 'be renewed, made larger, healthier'. Finally, in October 1915 he joined the 'Bantams', a special battalion for men who (like Rosenberg) were too short to be accepted into other regiments.

AT THE FRONT

Rosenberg later transferred to the King's Own Royal Lancasters and went to fight on the Somme in June 1916. Shortly afterwards, *August 1914* marked the beginning of his career as a war poet and chronicler of lice and rats as well as death and destruction. He was in and out of the front line for almost two years and, despite his absent-mindedness (he was frequently punished for offences such as forgetting his gas mask), proved himself a good soldier. But the strain eventually began to tell, and he confessed to Marsh that 'It is breaking me completely'. On 1 April 1918, during a fierce German offensive, Rosenberg lost his life. The sector was fought over for weeks afterwards, and his body was never recovered. His poems – which he had prudently sent, one by one, to Edward Marsh in London – survived him, to bring him belated fame for his outstanding gifts.

Painter's vision
At the age of 20, Rosenberg despaired 'of ever writing excellent poetry' and saw his future as an artist. Winning a place at the Slade School of Art was his open door into London's artistic circles, but he never earned a living with his landscapes (above) or portraiture. When he joined up, he no longer had the chance and materials to paint and was obliged to turn exclusively to poetry. He came to the conclusion that 'I am more deep and true as a poet than painter'.

Fighting Bantams
Rosenberg's small stature made him eligible for the Suffolk Bantams, a battalion of men too small to qualify elsewhere. He later joined the King's Own Royal Lancasters, and was killed at dawn on 1 April 1918, while on night patrol.

"DREAMS THAT DRIP WITH MURDER"

Romantic ideas of glory and chivalry which inspired the soldier-poets in 1914, turned to "dreams that drip with murder" and anger at the warmongering generals who sent young men to their deaths.

The English poetry of the First World War can be divided roughly into two periods. At its outbreak the poets celebrated the war, sharing with the mass of non-combatants a simple, heroic vision of noble sacrifice for one's country. But that naïve idealism died amid the appalling carnage of the Battle of the Somme in 1916.

By the end of the war millions of men had lost their lives in a deadlocked war of attrition on the Western Front. The young men who experienced it forged a new kind of poetry, poetry that for the first time faced up to the full horror of the war. These poems are brutal and direct, contemptuous of patriotic zeal on the Home Front, angry at the statesmen and generals who instigated the slaughter. 'My subject is War, and the pity of War', wrote Wilfred Owen.

The 1914–18 war was the first in which ordinary British civilians enlisted or were conscripted to fight. The soldiers who turned war into poetry were uniquely well-equipped to do so. Well-educated, predominantly from the middle and upper classes, they mostly served as junior officers, and as such had the job of leading their men into battle – the reason so many perished.

A profound bond developed among "Those who were there" on the Western Front. And though the war poets found little that was noble in war itself, there was much that was noble in the humour and bravery of their fellow soldiers.

PATRIOTIC VERSES

To the young poets and patriotic versifiers of 1914 the war had beckoned like a glorious adventure. In the first 18 months of the war more than two million men were borne to the recruiting stations on a wave of nationalistic fervour that found its most celebrated expression in the poems and person of Rupert Brooke. Educated at Rugby and Cambridge, Brooke had already made his mark as a poet by 1914. "Now, God be thanked Who has matched us with His hour", he wrote in *Peace*. Those who went to war for their country would do so "as swimmers into cleanness leaping". This accorded

Augustus John: Fraternity, Trustees of the Imperial War Museum

THE VETERAN'S FAREWELL.

"Good Bye, my lad, I only wish I were young enough to go with you!"

ENLIST NOW!

E.T. Archive

"Now, God be thanked Who has matched us with His hour,
And caught our youth, and wakened us from sleeping,
With hand made sure, clear eye, and sharpened power,
To turn, as swimmers into cleanness leaping."
FROM *PEACE* BY RUPERT BROOKE, 1914

---

with the wisdom of the hour: the war would be over in six months – it would be a clean victory.

Brooke saw very little active service. He died of acute blood poisoning in 1915 as he waited to take part in the Gallipoli landings, and was, according to Winston Churchill, 'all that one would wish England's noblest sons to be'.

Brooke's *Peace* belongs to a volume called *1914 Sonnets* that also contains his most anthologized poem, *The Soldier*, which was considered a perfect distillation of the national mood:

If I should die, think only this of me:
That there's some corner of a foreign field

"Recruiting"
(left) While patriotic posters urged the country's young men to "go and help", E. A. Mackintosh wrote with bitter irony "How the message ought to read": "Go and help them swell the names/In the casualty lists./Help to make a column's stuff/For the blasted journalists.

Brothers in arms
(above) The shared experience of war bred a profound sense of brotherhood among the soldiers. And the poems written by officers reveal how they came to feel as fathers for the men in their command. In In Memoriam, *E. A. Mackintosh wrote: "Oh, never will I forget you/My men that trusted me,/ More my sons than your fathers',/ For they could only see/ The little helpless babies/And the young men in their pride./ They could not see you dying,/ And hold you while you died."*

That is forever England. There shall be
* In that rich earth a richer dust concealed;*
A dust whom England bore, shaped,
*   made aware...*

There was scarcely a household that did not have occasion to seek consolation in Brooke's verses. Another poem that achieved symbolic popularity was John McCrae's *In Flanders Fields,* which first appeared anonymously in *Punch* in 1915:

In Flanders fields the poppies blow
Between the crosses, row on row
* That mark our place; and in the sky*
* The larks, still bravely singing, fly*
Scarce heard amid the guns below.

This poem is at least one reason why the British Legion chose the poppy as a symbol of remembrance for the war dead. The concluding lines read as a veiled warning against those who argued for a negotiated peace:

If ye break faith with us who die
We shall not sleep, though poppies grow
* In Flanders fields.*

One of the most skilled poems of this early mood of optimism and certainty is Julian Grenfell's *Into Battle.* Included in a letter home, it is remarkable for being the work of a professional soldier, one of the very few war poems written by an amateur poet to have stood the test of time.

Grenfell, the son of Lord Desborough, received the D.S.O. (Distinguished Service Order) for outstanding bravery. *Into Battle* was written early in 1915 and published in *The Times.* A few weeks later Grenfell was killed in action. The

"In Flanders fields..."
(above) Thriving in the churned earth of the Front, "Poppies whose roots are in man's veins" soon took on symbolic significance.

"They shall not return to us..."
Rudyard Kipling lost his son in the trenches (below). Life expectancy for officers such as Lieutenant Kipling was nine months.

poem does not appeal to patriotism or the righteousness of the cause. It simply hymns the glory of war and the fighting man:

The fighting man shall from the sun
* Take warmth, and life from the glowing*
*   earth;*
Speed with the light-foot winds to run,
* And with the trees to newer birth;*
And find, when fighting shall be done,
* Great rest, and fullness after dearth.*

While the newspapers continued to publish such idealizing verses and the recruiting posters urged noble sacrifice, the messy reality of war took grip on the men at the Front. In *In Memoriam,* E. A. Mackintosh expresses the gulf that was developing between the civilian population in England and the army in France, the contrast between flag-waving send-offs and the squalor of death:

Happy and young and gallant,
They saw their first-born go,
But not the strong limbs broken
And the beautiful men brought low...

His *Recruiting* contains a bitter attack on the armchair warriors:

Fat civilians wishing they
'Could go and fight the Hun.'
Can't you see them thanking God
That they're over forty-one?

E. A. Mackintosh was killed in action in 1917 after being gassed and wounded at the Somme the year before.

It was indeed the Battle – or rather the battles – of the Somme that blew away

87

forever any remaining romantic illusions regarding the war. On 1 July 1916 thousands of British and French troops poured from their trenches towards the German lines, and as they staggered across No Man's Land under the weight of heavy packs were cut to ribbons by machine gun fire. By nightfall an appalling 20,000 British troops were dead and 40,000 wounded – the heaviest loss sustained in a single day in the whole of the First World War. The carnage did not stop there. Wave after wave of monstrous, futile attacks continued on into the autumn, while heavy rains churned the battlefield into thick, treacherous mud. By the time of the last offensive, 13 November 1916, the British Expeditionary Force had lost 420,000 men, dead or seriously wounded.

This slaughter on Flanders fields deepened the determination of poets such as Siegfried Sassoon and Wilfred Owen to paint the war as it really was. Sassoon – educated, like Brooke, at Cambridge – was a fearless soldier who had received military honours for bravery. His unadorned language and conversational tone were still a novelty in poetry, as in these lines from *Counter-Attack*:

Things seemed all right at first. We held
their line,
With bombers posted, Lewis guns well placed,
And clink of shovels deepening the
shallow trench.
The place was rotten with dead. . .

The first of Sassoon's 'outspoken' war poems (as he called them), *In the Pink* (1917), was actually refused by *The Westminster* magazine since 'they thought it might prejudice recruiting!!' Sassoon's poetry became increasingly bitter and satirical, 'deliberately written to disturb complacency'. His principal targets were the politicians and newspaper leader writers who whipped the nation into a bellicose fury, and the civilians who could have no conception of what the troops endured at the Front. '*Blighters*' combines the anger and wit that characterized much of his poetry:

The House is crammed: tier beyond tier
they grin
And cackle at the Show, while prancing
ranks
Of harlots shrill the chorus, drunk with din;
'We're sure the Kaiser loves our dear
old Tanks!'

I'd like to see a Tank come down the stalls,
Lurching to ragtime tunes, or 'Home,
sweet Home',
And there'd be no more jokes in Music-halls
To mock the riddled corpses round Bapaume.

"Dulce et Decorum"

"Bent double, like old beggars under sacks . . . deaf even to the hoots of gas-shells dropping softly behind." In this poem, fine-sounding rhetoric about the glories of war – 'It is sweet and right to die for one's country' – is belied by the gruesome reality of the Front.

"In an Underground Dressing-Station"

The pain and terror of the wounded is brought into sharp focus in many poems – particularly Sassoon's: " 'O put my leg down, doctor, do!' (He'd got/A bullet in his ankle; and he'd been shot/ Horribly through the guts.)"

Sassoon believed the war was being needlessly prolonged by statesmen and brass hats who had it in their power to negotiate a settlement. In 1917, following the publication of his first book of war poems, *The Old Huntsman*, his revulsion at the continuing carnage reached a crisis point. 'As an act of wilful defiance of military authority' he prepared a statement for his commanding officer. 'I have seen and endured the sufferings of the troops', he wrote, 'and I can no longer be a party to prolong these sufferings for ends which I believe to be evil and unjust.' He was not court-martialled as he had expected and perhaps wished. Instead he was sent to the military hospital in Edinburgh. Here he met Wilfred Owen.

SASSOON AND OWEN

Asking Sassoon to autograph copies of *The Old Huntsman*, Owen shyly admitted that he, too, wrote poems. Sassoon was impressed with what he saw and their friendship soon developed into a deep literary bond. With the encouragement and advice of Sassoon, and fellow-poets Robert Graves and Robert Nichols, Owen began the series of poems (called, simply, *Poems*) which was to ensure his literary fame.

Owen had served in the trenches for the

> "Gas! Gas! Quick, boys! – An ecstasy of fumbling,
> Fitting the clumsy helmets just in time,
> But someone still was yelling out and stumbling
> And floundering like a man in fire or lime. –
> Dim through the misty panes and thick green light,
> As under a green sea, I saw him drowning."
>
> FROM *DULCE ET DECORUM EST* BY WILFRED OWEN,
> 1917-18

first half of 1917 before being invalided home wounded and shell-shocked. During this convalescence he carried about with him photographs of dead and dying men at the Front, which he would thrust wordlessly under the noses of back-slapping patriots who had the temerity to approach him.

Despite his profound opposition to the war he returned to the fighting in 1918 as a company commander. 'I came out in order to help these boys', he wrote to his mother, 'by watching their sufferings that I may speak of them as well as a pleader can.' In *Apologia pro Poemate Meo* ('A Defence of My Poetry'), which was written in response to a letter from Robert Graves telling Owen to 'cheer up and write more optimistically', he talks of the

bond he developed with his men, having shared "With them in hell the sorrowful dark of hell" and discovered that "These men are worth/ Your tears".

In October 1918 Wilfred Owen was awarded the Military Cross for outstanding bravery. The following month, just a week before the Armistice, he was killed in action. He was 25.

Cecil Day Lewis talked of Owen's 'unsentimental pity, his savage and sacred indignation'. Owen's achievement was in transmitting the horror of localized suffering, the terror of individual moments, into a more universal compassion. The opening of *Dulce et Decorum Est* ('It is Sweet and Right [to die for one's country]') – "Bent double, like old beggars under sacks,/ Knock-kneed, coughing

Devastation
Two years changed landscape and poetry totally: Grenfell's "naked earth . . . warm with spring . . . and bursting trees" (1915) becomes a "menacing scarred slope" in Sassoon's Attack *(1917).*

91

"Strange Meeting"

Compassion for the fallen German enemy (left) permeates Owen's Strange Meeting, *in which the poet meets, in hell, a soldier whom he has killed. After death, they make strange friends: "Whatever hope is yours,/Was my life also," the enemy-friend tells him.*

"Have you forgotten yet?"

In Aftermath, *written in 1919, Sassoon bids the reader to swear "by the green of the spring" never to forget the reality of war (below) – the "rats", "stench", "corpses rotting", and "the stretcher-cases lurching back/ With dying eyes and lolling heads – those ashen-grey/Masks of the lads who once were keen and kind and gay".*

people find my poems difficult', he wrote. For he used compressed language in a startlingly, original way. In *Returning, we hear the Larks*, birdsong penetrates the gloom and terror of night on the battlefield and delivers a strange, brief moment of exultation:

> *Death could drop from the dark*
> *As easily as song –*
> *But song only dropped,*
> *Like a blind man's dreams on the sand*
> *By dangerous tides;*
> *Like a girl's dark hair, for she dreams no*
> *ruin lies there,*
> *Or her kisses where a serpent hides.*

DETAILED HORROR

There is, too, a certain detachment about his poetry, an ability to record in minute but objective detail the horrors that took place around him. 'I will not leave a corner of my consciousness covered up, but saturate myself with the strange and extraordinary new conditions of this life', Rosenberg wrote to one of his mentors, Laurence Binyon. *Louse Hunting* records the "demons' pantomine" of soldiers trying to rid themselves and their clothing of the lice that were a bane of life in the trenches:

> *See the silhouettes agape,*
> *See the gibbering shadows*
> *Mixed with the baffled arms on the wall.*
> *See gargantuan hooked figures*
> *Pluck in supreme flesh*
> *To smutch supreme littleness.*

like hags, we cursed through sludge" – displays the kind of direct, unpoetic language he favoured. 'I don't want to write anything to which a soldier would say *No compris!*', he wrote to Sassoon. The poem progresses through a description of a gas attack to an image that haunts the mind:

> *If in some smothering dreams you too*
> *could pace*
> *Behind the wagon that we flung him in,*
> *And watch the white eyes writhing in his*
> *face,*
> *His hanging face, like a devil's sick of sin;*
> *. . . My friend, you would not tell with*
> *such high zest*
> *To children ardent for some desperate*
> *glory,*
> *The old Lie: Dulce et decorum est*
> *Pro patria mori.*

More than any other poem, *Strange Meeting* reveals Owen as a poet of genius – 'his passport to immortality', Sassoon called it. Its visionary quality – which owes a debt to the Romantic poets, especially Shelley – elevates it above the mass of war poetry, while its technical accomplishments are innovatory, the half-rhymes remorselessly evoking a disjointed world. The poem tells of the meeting – in a subterranean hell – of an English soldier and the German soldier he has killed:

> *'Strange friend,' I said, 'here is no cause*
> *to mourn.'*
> *'None,' said the other, 'save the undone years,*
> *The hopelessness. . .*

It contains a fitting epitaph for Owen's life and work:

> *. . . of my weeping something had been left,*
> *Which must die now. I mean the truth untold,*
> *The pity of war, the pity war distilled.*

Isaac Rosenberg's poetry is not a poetry of protest, as is Sassoon's, nor does it appeal to compassion, like Wilfred Owen's. Rosenberg called it 'an attempt to enrich the world of ideas'. 'Most

"Returning, we hear the Larks"
(left) Rosenberg evokes the beauty of the larks' song amid the destruction – "music showering on our upturned faces".

"Does it Matter?"
(right) Owen and Sassoon both wrote with angry irony about those wounded soldiers whose lives would be blighted by the war.

One of Rosenberg's finest poems – indeed one of the finest poems of the First World War – is _Dead Man's Dump_. It describes soldiers on mule-drawn carts ('limbers') carrying barbed wire to an advanced position. The wheels of the carts roll over the corpses of both English and German soldiers – "They lie there huddled, friend and foeman" – that litter their path. Again, the horror is recorded dispassionately:

> The wheels lurched over sprawled dead
> But pained them not, though their bones
> crunched;
> . . . A man's brains splattered on
> A stretcher-bearer's face:

As the poem moves towards its climax, so the limbers approach men who have only just died. One is still alive – "The blood-dazed intelligence" cries out "through the suspense of the far-torturing wheels". The limbers hasten to reach him, but they are too late:

> So we crashed round the bend,
> We heard his weak scream,
> We heard his very last sound,
> And our wheels grazed his dead face.

Rudyard Kipling was a very different kind of war poet from Rosenberg. At the outbreak of war the distinguished, middle-aged poet had obliged with some predictably patriotic outpourings. But with the death of his only son in 1915 – killed in action at Loos – Kipling's verses became deeply and bitterly angry. In _Mesopotamia_ he raises his voice on behalf of ordinary people, indignant at the faceless few sending their sons up the line to death:

> They shall not return to us, the resolute, the young,
> The eager and whole-hearted whom we gave:
> But the men who left them thriftily to lie in their own dung,
> Shall they come with years and honour to the grave?

Sometimes he pared his anger down to a sharp point of epigrammatic savagery, as in _Common Form_:

> If any question why we died,
> Tell them, because our fathers lied.

It was through Kipling's endowment that for many years the Last Post (taps) was sounded every night at the Ypres war memorial, the Menin Gate. A decade after

---

> **_"The air is loud with death,_**
> **_The dark air spurts with fire,_**
> **_The explosions ceaseless are._**
> **_Timelessly now, some minutes past,_**
> **_These dead strode time with vigorous life,_**
> **_Till the shrapnel called 'An end!'"_**
>
> FROM _DEAD MAN'S DUMP_
> BY ISAAC ROSENBERG, 1917

---

the end of the war a visit to this monument inspired Siegfried Sassoon to an eloquently brutal tribute to the millions who lost their lives:

> Who will remember, passing through this Gate,
> The unheroic Dead who fed the guns?
> Who shall absolve the foulness of their fate, –
> Those doomed, conscripted, unvictorious ones?
> Crudely renewed, the Salient holds its own.
> Paid are its dim defenders by this pomp;
> Paid, with a pile of peace-complacent stone,
> The armies who endured that sullen swamp.
>
> Here was the world's worst wound. And here with pride
> 'Their name liveth for ever,' the Gateway claims.
> Was ever an immolation so belied
> As these intolerably nameless names?
> Well might the Dead who struggled in the slime
> Rise and deride this sepulchre of crime.

THE FIRST WORLD WAR

**In a clash of rival imperialisms, the 'war to end wars'
claimed the lives of millions, devastated entire nations
and shattered the very idea of civilization.**

On the morning of 28 June 1914 Archduke Franz Ferdinand, heir apparent to the throne of Austria-Hungary, was shot dead as he was being driven through the streets of Sarajevo. His wife also died at the hands of the assassin, a Bosnian student named Gavrilo Princip. The crime naturally enough excited considerable comment, but it was not seen as a particular cause for alarm. Political assassination had been a regrettable feature of European life for a generation, and there had been several bungled attempts on members of the Hapsburg dynasty, which for centuries had been the ruling house in large parts of Central Europe. It was not surprising that one should finally succeed in the capital of the empire's volatile provinces of Bosnia-Hertzegovina.

The shooting at Sarajevo, however, had shattering consequences for the world. No single incident in modern history has had such repercussions. It set in train a sequence of events that led directly to war on a colossal scale. How could a couple of pistol shots in a provincial capital lead to such a catastrophe? Was it perversity on the part of key decision-makers? Or a general failure of the sophisticated European political system? Or somehow a consequence of the strains imposed by national competition and rivalry – with the murder of the Archduke merely the final straw?

A WEB OF ALLIANCES

The Great Powers, as the principal European states were then called, had by 1914 divided themselves into rival armed camps, each camp bound together by a complex web of mutual assistance treaties in case of attack. On the one side was the so-called Triple Alliance.

The leading member of the Triple Alliance was Kaiser Wilhelm II's Germany, by any measure the mightiest force in continental Europe. Allied to Germany, by ties of blood as well as self-

interest, was the ramshackle Austro-Hungarian Empire, with a comparatively lightweight Italy completing the trio. Against the Triple Alliance stood the Triple Entente: Russia, France, and a loosely attached Britain. Both sides had followed the now-familiar path of arming themselves to the teeth in order to protect themselves against the other.

Sarajevo provided the flashpoint because Austria-Hungary was being tormented by unrest in her Balkan possessions and by the existence of the independent kingdom of Serbia, which was the focal point for that unrest. Princip, for example, was a member of a terrorist organization which had close links with elements in the Serbian government, although the assassination plot was certainly not instigated or backed by the authorities in Belgrade. However, Austria-Hungary seized on the incident as an opportunity to settle scores with Serbia, once and for all. And Vienna was emboldened to do this by virtue of Kaiser Wilhelm's full-blooded support. The

Mary Evans Picture Library

Head-on collision
*Old territorial
rivalries and a
complex network of
treaties dragged
country after country
into the fighting.
The efforts of both
sides to drive home a
crippling early
offensive met head on
in Belgium and
France (right).
There was complete
stalemate.*

EUROPE

☐ Central powers

▨ Allied Powers

■ Neutral States

The Western Front
*Troops dug into
trenches which ran all
the way from the
Swiss border to the
sea (right). Sites of
any strategic value
were fought over
inconclusively for
months.*

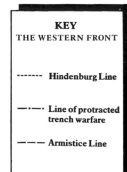

KEY
THE WESTERN FRONT

- - - - - - **Hindenburg Line**

- · - · - **Line of protracted
trench warfare**

- - - - **Armistice Line**

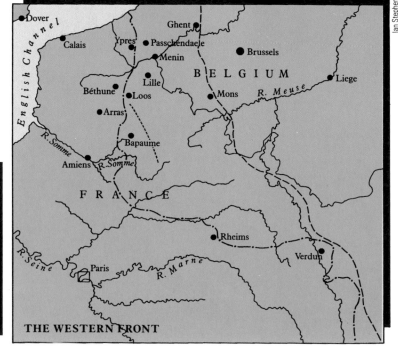

THE WESTERN FRONT

Ian Stephen

The first casualties

The assassination of Archduke Franz Ferdinand and his wife, pictured left minutes before their deaths, was the excuse for Austria-Hungary to bring Serbia into line. Kaiser Wilhelm (inset) adopted a belligerent stance, and had been arming steadily. Political truth – that 'first casualty of war' – gave way to ghoulish propaganda. The 'Hun's' spiked helmet was worn (British posters implied) only by rapists and baby-butchers (below). When the bottom picture was taken (Dec 1915), the Dardanelles campaign was in chaos; casualties were counted in daily thousands. These volunteers knew they stood every chance of being killed.

Key Dates

1914

28 June Archduke Franz Ferdinand assassinated

28 July Austria-Hungary declares war on Serbia

1 Aug Germany declares war on Russia

3 Aug Germany declares war on France and invades Belgium

4 Aug Britain declares war on Germany

5 Aug Austria-Hungary declares war on Russia

6 Aug Serbia declares war on Germany

10 Aug France declares war on Austria-Hungary

12 Aug Britain declares war on Austria-Hungary

6 Sept First Battle of Marne begins

27 Sept Russians invade Hungary

19 Oct First Battle of Ypres begins

3 Nov Russia declares war on Turkey

5 Nov Britain and France declare war on Turkey

1915

22 Apr Germans first use poison gas at Ypres

23 Apr Rupert Brooke dies in Greece

25 Apr Allied forces land at Gallipoli

30 Apr Julian Grenfell dies at Ypres

7 May U-boat sinks British *Lusitania*

23 May Italy declares war on Austria-Hungary

20 Aug Italy declares war on Turkey

15 Oct Britain declares war on Bulgaria

1916

21 Jan Robert Palmer killed in Mesopotamia

21 Feb Battle of Verdun begins

9 Mar Germany declares war on Portugal

31 May Battle of Jutland

1 July Allies launch Somme offensive; 60,000 British casualties on first day

28 Aug Italy declares war on Germany

8 Sept T. M. Kettle killed in action

1917

8 Mar Revolution begins in Russia

6 Apr USA declares war on Germany

9 Apr R. E. Vernède killed in action

31 July Passchendaele offensive begun by British

14 Aug China declares war on Germany and Austria-Hungary

Oct E. A. Mackintosh killed in action

5 Dec Russia and Germany sign armistice

7 Dec USA declares war on Austria-Hungary

1918

Jan John McCrae dies of pneumonia

3 Mar Treaty of Brest-Litovsk

1 Apr Isaac Rosenberg killed in action

22 July Allies cross Marne beginning decisive counter-offensive

4 Nov Wilfred Owen killed in action

9 Nov Kaiser Wilhelm II abdicates

11 Nov Germany and Allies sign armistice

The 'Lusitania'
The sinking of the
Lusitania *(left)*
damaged Germany's
propaganda war.
Many Americans
were among the dead,
which meant that
when the US joined
the war, it would be
on the Allied side.

view from Berlin was that Russia would not dare intervene to defend its Serbian friends and fellow Slavs, and by failing to do so would lose credibility as a Great Power. Guessing or predicting correctly is the key to successful diplomacy, and Europe was now entering a period of disastrously unsuccessful diplomacy.

DECLARATIONS OF WAR

On 23 July Austria-Hungary issued Serbia with a deliberately unacceptable set of demands, and declared war on the 28th. The next fateful decision was taken by Tsar Nicholas II. On the 30th, after his usual dithering, he ordered a general mobilization against both Austria-Hungary and Germany. On the 31st, Germany demanded that Russia stop mobilizing at once. Refusal was followed by Germany's declaration of war on Russia on

1 August. Two of the Great Powers were now formally at war. This was extremely alarming but not, surely, the point of no return for the whole of Europe? In fact it was to be so, because unknown to any of the others, Germany had an unalterable military plan in case of war with Russia.

Germany's greatest fear was war on two fronts simultaneously, and her plan was to deliver a quick knock-out blow against Russia's ally, France, before turning to the east to face the Russians.

France began mobilization on 1 August, and dismissed a German demand for neutrality – which Germany knew she was bound to do. On 3 August Germany declared war on France, and finally revealed the most dangerous element in her military strategy. This called for launching a massive assault on France, not directly, but indirectly by way of Bel-

gium, so as to sweep past the French defences and encircle her army.

Belgium's neutrality was guaranteed by Britain, and when Germany attacked Belgium on the 3rd, Britain demanded her immediate withdrawal. Germany had gambled that Britain would not come to France's aid, but that was suddenly irrelevant once Britain decided to make Belgian neutrality the issue.

There was now no way of turning back for anyone. Britain declared war on Germany on 4 August, and, rather belatedly, considering that they had set the whole horrifying process in operation, Austria-Hungary declared war on Russia the following day.

'OVER BY CHRISTMAS'
In such a seemingly careless way did the Great Powers of Europe find themselves at war. What sort of war did they expect it to be? Military experts and the public at large, on both sides, were, in general, agreed on one point: that there would be a short, sharp clash of modern, well-equipped armies, and victory would go to those employing the most imaginative strategies and displaying the finest fighting qualities. It would not last long. There was patriotic frenzy in all the European capitals during those heady days of early August. This carnival-like atmosphere

'Ils ne passeront pas!'
At Verdun (above), the French held, then turned the German advance – but at huge cost. General Nivelle rallied his demoralized troops with the cry: 'They shall not pass!'

Under fire
The startling beauty of the battlefield (right) long haunted men marooned in the trenches. Night was sometimes bright as day with artillery fire and flares, and the noise was incessant.

infected the soldiers too, as they dashed off to the Front. 'It'll be all over by Christmas', chanted the British. French troops chalked the swaggering slogan 'To Berlin!' on the railway wagons carrying them eastward. The German Crown Prince exulted in the prospect of a 'bright and jolly war'.

This frivolity was to be short-lived. The British Foreign Secretary Sir Edward Grey, as he gazed out of his window at the cheering throng on the evening of 3 August remarked, 'The lamps are going out all over Europe; we shall not see them lit again in our lifetime.'

In some respects, the opening hostilities lived up to those expectations of rapid movement and decisive battles. The German armies swept through Belgium as planned, driving the outnumbered British Expeditionary Force (BEF)

before it (the retreat from Mons, begun on 24 August). The momentum of the invasion carried the Germans well into northern France, but in one of the most critical battles ever fought, the French and British stopped the German advance at the Battle of the Marne (6-12 September).

A second German attempt to achieve a quick victory in the west was thwarted by the BEF, reinforced by the French, at Ypres. Fighting began in October and lasted into the first half of November. Ypres effectively brought the war in the west to a stalemate, as both sides dug themselves into a line of trenches stretching unbroken from the Swiss border to the English Channel. In the east, meanwhile, early Russian advances against the Austrians and into East Prussia had been halted, and at the Battle of Tannenberg (26-30 August) the Germans had dealt the Russians a shattering blow.

By Christmas 1914, therefore, the war had settled into the pattern that would remain little changed for four dreadful years. On the Eastern Front the beleaguered Russians dug themselves in, stoically enduring the most appalling hardships until the Tsarist regime crumbled in 1917. On the Western Front, the full horror of trench warfare began to unfold, as equally matched forces tried either to get round or smash through the trench barrier.

TOTAL DEADLOCK

This stalemate came as an unwelcome surprise to everyone. Even the politicians and the generals had badly misread the true state of modern warfare and modern industrial society. They had not understood the colossal destructive power of the weaponry at their disposal. Machine guns, magazine rifles and barbed wire were a deadly enough combination to hold back any infantry advance, no matter

To the slaughter
Starting out full of bravado (left), troops found themselves in hell: facing death, in mires like Passchendaele, below.

BBC Hulton Picture Library

Mansell Collection

End of the line
The horrors of the trenches were manifold: lice, trench foot (a gangrenous condition), a shortage of ammunition, filth, lack of privacy, dead bodies, rats and mud, fear of sniper attacks and of the next order to go 'over the top'. But comradeship flourished among the men.

how much human fodder was thrown into it. The only possible way to attack with any hope of success was to pulverize the enemy position in advance by artillery bombardment. But with massive reinforcements ready to be called up to hold the line, even successful assaults meant no more than capturing a few hundred yards of ground.

Neither had anyone grasped the phenomenal war-making capacity of industrial societies. Because nothing remotely like it had ever happened before, it was not imagined possible that entire nations could be organized so as to wage war totally. Never before had entire societies been pitched into war against each other, with every aspect of organized human life directed towards pouring men and material into conflict. No matter how war-weary the civilian populations became, they never slackened their effort.

FURTHER INVOLVEMENT
As the truth sank in, the question was what to do about it. Undefeated nations at war do not lay down their arms simply because they discover the cost of war to be higher than they imagined it to be. In the First World War the nations involved redoubled their efforts.

From the beginning, the protagonists

had searched for new allies in order to tilt the scales. Soon after the outbreak of war, Japan took the side of the Allies (as Britain, France and Russia were known), while the decaying Ottoman Empire sided with the Central Powers (Germany and Austria-Hungary). Italy, although a member of the original Triple Alliance, opted for neutrality in 1914 and then joined the Allies the following year. Smaller European states became embroiled too: Bulgaria on the side of the Central Powers; Rumania, Greece and Portugal on the side of the Allies. The fact that Britain was involved meant that the entire British Empire was at war – most notably the Old Dominions, who rushed to the aid of the Mother Country.

In military terms, the deadlock reached at the end of 1914 resulted in two broad strategies. The generals on both sides believed that the only way out of the impasse was to throw more and more men and armaments into the fray. Something, somewhere, was bound to give sooner or later. It might (and did) cost millions of lives, but that was the only way of preventing defeat. Such military obstinacy prevailed to the bitter end.

The other strategy was to make warfare so frightful that the other side would not be able to sustain it. In battlefield terms it

meant devising evermore heinous weapons of destruction – the German introduction of poison gas was the most notorious example. More broadly, there was a concerted onslaught by both sides on the morale, health and even lives of the enemy civilian populations, chiefly by starving them into submission.

THE WAR AT SEA
In the years leading up to the war, Germany had made a great effort to get on level terms with the British navy. She had failed in this, and after one major if inconclusive sea battle (Jutland, 31 May 1916), the German fleet never sailed again. Britain's naval superiority meant that she could mount an effective blockade of Germany. Germany, for her part, possessed in the U-Boat a new weapon of remarkable effectiveness. In early 1915 Germany began attacking neutral shipping with U-Boats in an attempt to deprive Britain of food. Both blockades were the subject of intense propaganda campaigns, as each side tried to persuade the outside world of the other's barbarity.

The main target of this propaganda was the United States, which had declined to be drawn into the European quarrel but was becoming increasingly sympathetic to the Allied cause. This was particularly so over the matter of U-Boat attacks, and when the British liner *Lusitania* was torpedoed off the Irish coast on 7 May 1915 with the loss of 1200 lives, many of them Americans, it was clear that a continuation of this policy would provoke the United States beyond endurance. Germany drew back from this prospect – for the time being.

CEASELESS SLAUGHTER
Throughout 1915 and 1916 the slaughter on both the Eastern and Western Fronts continued remorselessly. The casualty figures were such as to beggar belief. The French army, for example, had lost 300,000 dead by the end of 1915. But that terrible total was more than doubled by the fighting before Verdun, which raged for most of the following year. Nearly as many Germans died at Verdun. At the same time, further north on the Somme, the British and Germans suffered about 400,000 casualties on either side. On the first day of the Battle of the Somme (1 July 1916) the British army lost 20,000 dead and twice that number wounded – all this in a single day.

There seemed no way to end the carnage. In 1915 the Allies attacked Turkey at the Dardanelles, attempting to knock her out of the way and thereby establish a

Back at home
Though civilians were largely ignorant of what the troops were suffering, they were not free from danger. Hundreds died in explosions at armament factories (left). Because of the shortage of men, women swelled the workforce, their war efforts giving them a new political voice.

THE WAR ARTISTS

Visions of war
John Singer Sargent,
fashionable portrait-
painter, showed
another side to his
talents when faced
with the horrors of
war. His vast frieze
Gassed (above),
showing soldiers
blinded by gas, is one
of the most famous of
all war paintings.
Stanley Spencer,
who served with the
Medical Corps in
Macedonia, set this
scene in a dressing
station in a Greek
church (below).

Painters as well as poets documented the conflict at the Fronts. Unlike the poets, however, some had the chance to work on an official footing. The British Government realized that visual records of the war could have great propaganda value, and in 1916 launched the Official War Artists scheme. Many artists were already on active service; there was even a regiment called the Artists' Rifles. Now several were recruited to chronicle the war.

The Ministry of Information, which ran the scheme, was advised by a committee drawn from the art world and public life. The first artist to be commissioned was Muirhead Bone, a distinguished draughtsman and etcher, who left for France on 16 August 1916 with the rank of Honorary 2nd Lieutenant. He toured the Front in a chauffeur-driven car and, by early October, had sent back 150 drawings showing various aspects of war and life behind the lines.

Many others followed, including some of the best-known artists of the day. These included men already serving, such as Paul Nash, and others too old for active service. Their works varied enormously in style and quality and included the celebration of war's dynamism as well as poignant indictments of its cruelties, and sober, factual records. One large group was made up of portraits of fighting men – from Field Marshals to common soldiers.

William Orpen
'The last thing I
want is to make
money out of the
sights I have seen',
wrote Orpen
(below). Based at
Amiens, he watched
men come back from
the Front 'wounded,
worn, sad and dirty'.
He was acutely
aware of his
privileged, protected
position:
'There I sat in the
car . . . and they
walked past in the
other direction to
Hell . . .'

Unquiet graves
Fighting crossed and re-crossed the same area, where the fallen lay buried (left).

'Dear Dada'
(below) This card was sent to a corporal in the BEF. It says: 'I am a good boy and waiting for you to come home . . .'

be able to come to Britain's rescue in time. As food shortages became increasingly acute in war-weary Britain, there seemed every chance that the gamble might work. The United States did declare war on Germany in April, but in the short term that could have no effect.

Even more serious for the Allies was the collapse of Tsarist Russia, the seizure of power by the Bolsheviks under Lenin and his immediate move to take Russia out of the war completely (December 1917). This meant that Germany could now throw her entire weight against the western Allies and the newly arriving Americans. Even without that, the situation on the Western Front had passed beyond redemption. A series of mutinies racked the exhausted French army, while in a number of bloody battles referred to collectively as Passchendaele, the British gained a few miles of churned up mud and blood – at the cost of 400,000 casualties.

direct link with Russia through the Black Sea. The attempt failed, as did the attempt to achieve anything decisive on the Balkan front at Salonika.

The situation became even worse from the Allies' point of view in 1917. Germany was desperate to force Britain out of the war before the British blockade in turn forced her out. The unrestricted submarine campaign began again. The Germans were gambling that the Americans, even if they came into the war, would not

Hostilities ended
The Armistice was signed (below) on 11 November 1918. About nine million combatants and thousands of civilians lay dead. Cities and economies were in ruins and few families in Europe were left unscathed.

A FATAL STRATEGY

As the horrific death toll in the trenches mounted there was widespread criticism of the strategy adopted and persisted in by the military commanders, such as General, later Field-Marshall, Sir Douglas Haig. His unflinching determination to smash the BEF up against the German defences implied an almost fatalistic disregard for the scale of casualties. The sickening slaughter at Passchendaele was perhaps the best case in point, and the British Prime Minister, David Lloyd George, was once heard to mutter, 'Blood and mud, they can think of nothing better!'

By the spring of 1918 Europe was nearly prostrate, although the armies in the field were as large and combative as ever. But for the first time since the autumn of 1914, the war took on a sense of movement. The Germans threw everything they had into one final assault on the Western Front. The Allies and Americans held, and as they counterattacked strongly it signalled the end. Understandably, the sight of well-fed, eager American troops, heralding the arrival of millions more, shook the morale of the Central Powers.

First Turkey and then Austria-Hungary began to disintegrate, and as revolutionary chaos threatened the existence of Germany, the Kaiser abdicated on 9 November. On the 11th, a new German government signed an armistice agreement with the Allies. At the cost of 9 million dead, an incalculable cost in terms of brute physical destruction, and an equally incalculable cost in terms of the sufferings of hundreds of millions of survivors, the war was over.

1914-1918

GERMANY	2,000,000	ITALY	460,000	
RUSSIA	1,700,000	TURKEY	375,000	
FRANCE	1,358,000	Br.EMPIRE	252,000	
AUSTRIA-HUNGARY	1,100,000	U.S.A	114,900	
GREAT-BRITAIN	761,000			

THE SIGNING OF THE ARMISTICE.

BIBLIOGRAPHY

Aers, David, *Chaucer, Langland and the Creative Imagination*. Routledge, Chapman & Hall (New York, 1980)

Angeli, H. R., *Shelley and His Friends in Italy* (reprint of 1911 edition). Haskell Booksellers (Brooklyn, 1972)

Baker, Jeffrey, *John Keats and Symbolism*. St. Martins's Press (New York, 1986)

Bloom, Harold, *Edmund Spenser*. Chelsea House (New York, 1986)

Brandl, Alois, *Samuel Taylor Coleridge and the English Romantic School* (reprint of 1887 edition). Haskell Booksellers (Brooklyn, 1969)

Cameron, Kenneth N., *Shelley: The Golden Years*. Harvard University Press (Cambridge, 1974)

Cantor, Paul A., *Creature and Creator: Myth-Making and the English Romanticism*. Cambridge University Press (New York, 1985)

Chute, Marchette, *Shakespeare of London*. E. P. Dutton (New York, 1957)

Darton, F. Harvey, *From Surtees to Sassoon: Some English Contrasts 1838-1928*. Folcroft Library Editions (Folcroft, 1931)

Delany, Paul, *The Neo-Pagans: Rupert Brooke and the Ordeal of Youth*. Free Press (New York, 1987)

Dickstein, Morris, *Keats and His Poetry: A Study in Development*. University of Chicago Press (Chicago, 1974)

Enscoe, Gerald, *Eros and the Romantics*. Mouton de Gruyter (Hawthorne, 1967)

Fussell, Paul, ed., *Siegfried Sassoon's Long Journey: Selections from the Sherston Memoirs*. Oxford University Press (New York, 1983)

Gardner, John C., *The Life and Times of Chaucer*. Alfred Knopf (New York, 1977)

Giddings, Robert, *The War Poets: The Lives and Writings of Rupert Brooke, Siegfried Sassoon, Wilfred Owen, Robert Graves, Edmund Blunden and the Other Great Poets of the 1914-1918 War*. Crown (New York, 1988)

Goldsworthy, W. Lansdown, *Ben Jonson and the First Folio*. Folcroft Library Editions (Folcroft, 1939)

Gordon, John D., *William Wordsworth, 1770-1850*. Folcroft Library Editions (Folcroft, 1950)

Halliday, F. E., *Shakespeare*. Thames & Hudson (New York, 1986)

Hamilton, Paul, *Coleridge's Poetics*. Stanford University Press (Stanford, 1983)

Hassall, Christopher, *Rupert Brooke: A Biography*. Faber & Faber (Winchester, 1972)

Henson, H. H., *Byron*. Haskell Booksellers (Brooklyn, 1974)

Hibberd, Dominic, *Owen the Poet*. University of Georgia Press (Athens, 1986)

Hills, Patricia, *John Singer Sargent*. Harry N. Abrams (New York, 1986)

Howard, Donald R., *Chaucer: His Life, His Works, His World*. E. P. Dutton (New York, 1987)

Keegan, John, *Biography of Siegfried Sassoon*. Viking Penguin (New York, 1987)

Knight, William, *The Life of William Wordsworth* (reprint of 1939 edition). Arden Library (Darby, 1978)

Mayhead, Robin, *John Keats*. Cambridge University Press (New York, 1967)

Peck, Walter E., *Shelley: His Life and Work* (reprint of 1927 edition). Burt Franklin (New York, 1969)

Pirie, David, *William Wordsworth: The Poetry of Grandeur and of Tenderness*. Routledge, Chapman & Hall (New York, 1982)

Pratt, Willis S., *Lord Byron and His Circle*. Haskell Booksellers (Brooklyn, 1970)

Roe, Nicholas, *Wordsworth and Coleridge: The Radical Years*. Oxford University Press (New York, 1988)

Russell, John, *Francis Bacon*. Thames & Hudson (New York, 1985)

Simcox, Kenneth, *Wilfred Owen: Anthem for a Doomed Youth*. Biblio Distribution Center (Totowa, 1988)

Smith, Godwin, *Shakespeare the Man*. Haskell Booksellers (Brooklyn, 1977)

Spender, Harold, *Byron and Greece* (reprint of 1924 edition). Richard West (Philadelphia, 1973)

Stallworthy, John, *Wilfred Owen*. Oxford University Press (New York, 1975)

Stopes, C. C., *Shakespeare's Sonnets* (reprint of 1904 edition). Richard West (Philadelphia, 1978)

Stopes, Charlotte, *Burbage and Shakespeare's Stage* (reprint of 1913 edition). Haskell Booksellers (Brooklyn, 1970)

Summerson, J., *Inigo Jones*. Longwood Publishing Group (Wolfeboro, 1964)

Tuckwell, William, *Chaucer* (reprint of 1904 edition). Richard West (Philadelphia, 1979)

INDEX